DISCIPLESHIP OF
THE HEART

Joe Holman

ISBN: 978-1-7366850-1-3

This book is dedicated to my wife, Denise. She is my role model and the best example of living out the material in this book. She is who I want to be when I grow up.

CONTENTS

Title Page

Copyright

Dedication

Another Book On Discipleship   1

I Am Right Here   3

God With Me   9

Abide In Christ   17

Holy Spirit   30

Spiritual Fruit   38

Tail Wagging The Dog   49

Disciplines Make Disciples   55

Do Everything   62

The Word   68

Giving   75

Prayer   84

Fasting   92

God Really Does Love Me   99

Known By Our Love   113

Think Right   128

Pure Heart   135

Wisdom   141

Humility   149

Grace   156

Faith   162

Evangelism   168

Discipling Others   175

Discipleship of the Heart Study Guide   180

God With Me   182

Abide In Me   183

Holy Spirit   184

Spiritual Fruit   185

Tail Wagging The Dog   186

Disciplines Make Disciples   187

Do Everything   188

The Word   189

Giving   190

Prayer   191

Fasting   192

God Really Does Love Me   193

Unconditional Love   194

Think Right   195

Pure Heart   196

Wisdom   197

Humility   198

Grace   199

Faith   200

Evangelism   201

Discipling Others   202

About The Author   203

ANOTHER BOOK ON DISCIPLESHIP

Welcome to another book about discipleship. Sound boring? It should. I mean, seriously, who needs another one of these? I just googled the word, "Discipleship". Search results tell me there are 17,200,000 pages. I put "Discipleship" in the search bar of Amazon with over 10,000 results.

So, why waste time on the 10,001 book? Why add my site and make 17,200,001? I have an excellent answer for you.

Look around. Read social media. Go to church.

How many disciples of Jesus can you easily identify?

How can we have so many books on discipleship and be so mean to people who disagree with our choice of politician?

How can we have over 17,000,000 pages to help us grow while every major denomination in the USA has decreased in numbers for almost two decades?

Where are all the people using these resources?

I am not being judgmental. I point out a discrepancy. It appears the church is doing a poor job of making disciples based upon a simple glance at culture and church.

I think we need to rethink the ideal of discipleship. It is time to go deeper than a Bible study or small group. We need to stop discipling our actions and begin with our hearts.

Welcome to another book about discipleship, but one which I hope is different. I hope it helps you look at who you are more than what you do. Welcome to Discipleship of the Heart. My goal is for our hearts to follow Jesus. This book is meant to be a shared journey. It is designed to be read together and talked about. I hope you do that.

I AM RIGHT HERE

"Daddy, look at me!"

As a father of eleven children, I cannot tell you how many times I have heard that statement. My children are doing something, and they want me to be a part of it. They want me to see them. They want me to affirm them. There is something about the presence of a parent that impacts a child.

I taught all of my children to ride a bike. Invariably, I would comfort them by saying, "I am right here. I have you. I will not let you fall." They were scared, but the fact I was right beside them gave them the courage they needed to try. They would always end up falling down. It is part of learning. When they fell, I would be there to pick them up. We would look at the bike and I would have them spit on it. Seriously, dad and me spitting on the bike put it back in its place. It could not beat us. We would spit, then I wiped the dirt off of them and off we went again.

I was with my children in the Amazon Jungle Basin. We were in a rainforest village doing ministry and building a church. It was around 3 in the morning and my five-year-old daughter woke me up. She had to go to the bathroom. The bathroom was anywhere not in the tent. We tried to not leave the tent after dusk because of the mosquitos. She insisted this was not an option. I took her to the edge of the camp. We heard something in the forest. It was a wild pig. I recognized the grunting. Her imagination made everything worse and scarier than normal. Wide-eyed, she tried to see into the darkness of the jungle at night. In fear, she reached out and took my hand. I told her it was okay. She had nothing to fear. I was with her. She looked at me and then all the fear just faded away. She knew dad would protect her.

As a parent, have you ever walked into a room and instantly see the behavior of your children change? Perhaps they were arguing or being mean to each other before you walked in on them. The moment they see you are in the room with them, their behavior changed. They knew their actions were unacceptable in the presence of their parent.

These are a few of the thousands of examples that you and I could talk about concerning the presence of a parent. Children are secure and brave when mom or dad are with them. Children behave better if they know their parents are there. Children seek to impress their parents.

I am writing a book on discipleship. It is going to differ from most books. I hope it is insightful and helps you grow. My main objective is to help you discover the key to discipleship is God.

I have been engaged in discipleship since I became a Christian in college back in 1982. The man who led me to Christ started discipling me the very next week. Discipleship has been in my spiritual DNA. Through individual and small group discipleship courses, I believe I have discipled over 300 people. I have used almost every discipleship program available for purchase and written my own. In the process of almost 4 decades of discipleship, I have I discovered something missing. The missing thing is not a small matter. It is not inconsequential. The missing component of my discipleship was God.

We have four children living at home with us. One of the favorite things for my daughters to do is play with Playdough. However, since we live in the Andes Mountains of Bolivia, we cannot get it. Sometimes it is available in a few stores, but when this happens, we have one or two options. We can buy Playdough, or we can eat. It is expensive. They should change the name to Play-gold.

At least once or twice a year I travel to the States for conferences and/or speaking engagements. These always provide me an opportunity to bring things back to Cochabamba. I take my clothes in a carryon and then two empty suitcases with me to fill up with goodies for the trip home. On one of my visits, I surprised the girls with Playdough. So, I brought home 10 pounds of Playdough and accessories. My daughters were ecstatic. They would get the Play-dough molds, put in the dough and just laugh and play when it would come out, shaped as a face, butterfly, teapot, or whatever. They loved cutting Play-dough hair and growing Play-dough beards.

As they were playing with their new toys, something dawned on me. Most of us live our Christian lives as if we were Play-dough People. Discipleship programs are the molds, and when we come out of the mold, we are all the same. I have been to church in every part of the United States and churches in France, Romania, Ghana, Mexico, and Bolivia. I have taken part in church services in over 20 languages. I am currently the pastor of a church in Bolivia made up predominantly of people from an Andean origin.

I discovered something interesting. No matter where you go, all the churches appear the same. They have the same program: Greeting, announcements, music, offering, three-point sermon, invitation, and closing prayer. They sing the same songs, just translated into other languages. There are a few exceptions, but as a general rule the only thing different is the language itself. I talked to pastors and leaders on five continents about discipleship, and it doesn't matter where you are; it is the same.

Read your Bible

Pray.

Go to church.

Try to get other people to read their Bible, pray, go to church and try to get other people to continue the process.

This is a very simplistic representation, but it is accurate. A disciple has a quiet time that comprises Bible reading and prayer. A disciple is an active member of a local church. A disciple evangelizes and disciples other. Discipleship is reading your Bible, praying, going to church, and trying to get other people to read their Bible, pray and go to church. This is the formula of discipleship. I said something was missing, and it was God. Where is God in our discipleship?

Christian discipleship has become little more than behavior modification. The goal is for people to fit the mold. We want them to act, dress and talk like us. We want them to do the same things we do in the same way we do them. Our goal is to create copies, but somewhere along the way we lost the original. We are making copies of copies of copies, and no one ever stops to ask about the original. We want to push the lever and the Christian behavior come out. Christians vote for this political party, take part in this activity, and go to these types of places.

We declared we are no longer under the Law while teaching our disciples to live under our new law. Our formula is the rule of life.

Over the years as I took and then led various discipleship courses and focused on discipleship in my churches, I kept sensing in my spirit there was something more. I taught these men and women how to read their Bibles, pray, go to church and get others to read their Bibles, pray and go to church. I made a lot of disciples. I also failed in the same task. My success was my failure. I helped many people change their behavior. I do not think I made disciples or followers of Christ. I helped people follow whichever particular system or book we were using. Teaching people to follow a system does not mean I helped them follow Jesus.

You are holding this book in your hand because you want to be a disciple. What does it mean? How can you tell if you are a good disciple? Is it because you met the super low standard of reading your Bible, praying, going to church and trying to get others to do this too? Did the first century disciples turn the world upside down by following our four-step discipleship program? What is a good disciple? How do you become one? What do you do? How do you know if you are a success in discipling or being discipled?

It is straightforward. A disciple is a follower of Christ. There are two components to it.

Go therefore and make disciples of all the nations, baptizing them in the name of the Father and the Son and the Holy Spirit, teaching them to observe all that I commanded you; and lo, I am with you always, even to the end of the age. (Matthew 28:19-20)

The first component is the focus of discipleship programs. We evangelize people, baptize them, and teach them basic Bible doctrine. The more intense discipleship programs teach more doctrine. Bible colleges and seminaries teach more doctrine. The focus is always on teaching. This makes us miss the second component.

The second part of the Great Commission is the heart of discipleship. *I am with you always, even to the end of the age.* The heart of being a follower of Christ is... now this will be so deep... **the heart of being a follower of Christ is following Christ.**

A disciple is someone who follows Christ. A discipler is someone who helps others follow Christ. A true disciple does not follow systems, rules, or a behavior modification method. A real disciple follows Jesus.

We ignore this in our discipleship and in our teaching. We relegate Jesus to history. He lived, died and rose again. These happened in the Bible times. Now, we follow His teachings in the present. Notice Jesus did not tell us to remember He was once here. He emphasized He is here. He said we are to observe all He commanded us, and HE was always with us. I am to follow the teacher, not the lesson plan.

A disciple is someone who follows Jesus and does what He tells them to do. I want to emphasize this. Someone who follows JESUS and does what HE tells them to do. The focus of being a disciple and of being a disciple maker is the Presence and Person of Jesus Christ.

A couple of theological terms describe the point I am making. The omnipresence of God teaches us God is 'all present'. God is present. He is fully present. God does not spread out over space and time. He is present in every sense of the word and in every place all the time. The immanence of God takes the omnipresence of God and adds something to it. It tells us that God is not merely present, He is active in His creation. God is present, and He is at work. That sentence is true for all people in all places during all times. As you read this sentence, I do not know where you are. I know this. God is present, and He is at work right there where you are. At the same moment, God is present, and He is at work here with me.

The next chapter focuses on this aspect. The truth I now hammer into those I mentor is God is here. We live in the Presence and Person of God. He leads us. We follow Him.

I missed this in the first thirty years of discipling others. I now focus on it.

I do not want to teach you what Jesus said. I want to help you hear what He is saying.

I don't want you to understand what Jesus did. I want to know what He is doing.

I do not want you to learn about the works He performed. I want to help you take part in the work He is performing.

Discipleship is not focused on the past and where Jesus walked. It is focused on the present and where He is taking you as He walks.

A disciple is not someone who studied what Jesus did. A disciple is someone who follows Jesus (now) and does what He tells them to do (now).

I discovered it is the Person and Presence of Jesus that changes everything. He is not a subject to study. He is the Lord to follow. It is all about Jesus. This truth is so simple yet profound. One of my favorite Bible verses sums it up like this:

But I am afraid that, as the serpent deceived Eve by his craftiness, your minds will be led astray from the simplicity and purity of devotion to Christ. (2 Corinthians 11:3)

Following Jesus is not complex. Don't be led astray from the simplicity and purity of devotion to Christ.

GOD WITH ME

I pastored a church in Virginia. One night during dinner I received a phone call from a leader in my church. I discovered it was a pocket call. He did not mean to dial me. I was calling his name, hoping he would hear me, in order to joke with him about the call. Then I realized what I was hearing. He was having an argument with his wife. I admit, I was torn between quickly hanging up and eavesdropping. I chose to hang up. Just as I disconnected, I heard him say my name. "Pastor Joe? Hello?" He saw our connection. He knew I could hear him. His voice tone, demeanor and attitude all changed. He went from speaking in a loud, almost yelling voice, to the soft-spoken man we all knew at church. I told him I thought he made a pocket call and was about to hang up. The following Sunday he asked me about the call. I confessed I heard him fighting. I told him I only heard a few seconds and was hanging up when he realized we were connected. He apologized to me. He was a good friend, and we went through the material comprising this book together. That allowed me to take the opportunity to speak into his life. I lovingly told him he did not need to apologize to me. Based on what I heard, he needed to ask his wife for forgiveness. He agreed and told me he asked her shortly after the phone call. He said he was embarrassed over the fact I had heard them. I told him before I ever heard a word, God was listening and watching the entire conflict. He understood because we had studied the Person and Presence of God together. My point is not a leader in my church argued with his wife. It is he stopped arguing with her when he realized I could hear him. The moment he saw Pastor Joe was listening to him, his actions and words changed. He did not want me to hear how he spoke to his wife when no one was around.

What would you do differently right now if you knew God was with you? How would you respond to someone if God were with you in the room? How would you handle temptation to sin if God had His hand on your shoulder at the moment of temptation? Would the Presence and Person of God impact your spending decisions? Your choice of words? Your actions?

This is my point, and it is also the focus of the Great Commission, the Bible and my life. God is here. It is such an important thing to know that God included it in the announcement of the Incarnation of Jesus.

"Behold, the virgin shall be with Child and shall bear a Son and they shall call His name, Immanuel, which translated means, 'God with us.'" (Matthew 1:23)

In Jesus, God is literally with us. The Holy Spirit actually lives inside of us! God is with us. Look at some verses just to get the feel of how incredibly important this truth is to the believer.

Now it came about at that time that Abimelech and Phicol, the commander of his army, spoke to Abraham, saying, "God is with you in all that you do; (Genesis 21:22)

"Sojourn in this land and I will be with you and bless you, for to you and to your descendants I will give all these lands, and I will establish the oath which I swore to your father Abraham." (Genesis 26:3)

"They said, 'We see plainly that the Lord has been with you'; so we said, 'Let there now be an oath between us, even between you and us, and let us make a covenant with you,'" (Genesis 26:28)

"Then the Lord said to Jacob, 'Return to the land of your fathers and to your relatives, and I will be with you.'" (Genesis 31:3)

"Then Israel said to Joseph, 'Behold, I am about to die, but God will be with you, and bring you back to the land of your fathers.'" (Genesis 48:21)

*"And He said, 'Certainly **I will be with you**, and this shall be the sign to you that it is I who have sent you: when you have brought the people out of Egypt, you shall worship God at this mountain.'" (Exodus 3:12)*

*He has not observed misfortune in Jacob; Nor has He seen trouble in Israel; **The Lord his God is with him**, And the shout of a king is among them. (Numbers 23:21)*

*"For the Lord your God has blessed you in all that you have done; He has known your wanderings through this great wilderness. These forty years the **Lord your God has been with you;** you have not lacked a thing." (Deuteronomy 2:7)*

*"The Lord is the one who goes ahead of you; **He will be with you**. He will not fail you or forsake you. Do not fear or be dismayed." (Deuteronomy 31:8)*

*"Then He commissioned Joshua the son of Nun, and said, "Be strong and courageous, for you shall bring the sons of Israel into the land which I swore to them, and **I will be with you**." (Deuteronomy 31:23)*

*"No man will be able to stand before you all the days of your life. Just as I have been with Moses, **I will be with you;** I will not fail you or forsake you." (Joshua 1:5)*

*"Have I not commanded you? Be strong and courageous! Do not tremble or be dismayed, for **the Lord your God is with you** wherever you go." (Joshua 1:9)*

*"And David said, 'The Lord who delivered me from the paw of the lion and from the paw of the bear, He will deliver me from the hand of this Philistine.' And Saul said to David, 'Go, and may the **Lord be with you**.'" (1 Samuel 17:37)*

*"Then Nathan said to David, 'Do all that is in your heart, for **God is with you**.'" (1 Chronicles 17:2)*

"Then David said to his son Solomon, 'Be strong and courageous, and

*act; do not fear nor be dismayed, for **the Lord God, my God, is with you**. He will not fail you nor forsake you until all the work for the service of the house of the Lord is finished.'" (1 Chronicles 28:20)*

*"Devise a plan, but it will be thwarted; State a proposal, but it will not stand, For **God is with us**." (Isaiah 8:10)*

*"When you pass through the waters, **I will be with you**; And through the rivers, they will not overflow you. When you walk through the fire, you will not be scorched, Nor will the flame burn you." (Isaiah 43:2)*

*"teaching them to observe all that I commanded you; and lo, **I am with you always**, even to the end of the age." (Matthew 28:20)*

*"I will ask the Father, and He will give you another Helper, that **He may be with you forever**;" (John 14:7)*

*"Now the **God of peace be with you** all. Amen." (Romans 15:33)*

*"Now may the Lord of peace Himself continually grant you peace in every circumstance. **The Lord be with you** all!" (2 Thessalonians 3:16)*

*"Make sure that your character is free from the love of money, being content with what you have; for He Himself has said, "**I will never desert you, nor will I ever forsake you**," (Hebrews 13:5)*

Look at how Jesus emphasized the relationship of God with His Children. It is one of such closeness God is literally inside of us and we are in Him.

I will ask the Father, and He will give you another Helper, so that He may be with you forever; the Helper is the Spirit of truth, whom the world cannot receive, because it does not see Him or know Him; but you know Him because He remains with you and will be in you. I will not leave you as orphans; I am coming to you. After a little while, the world no longer is going to see Me, but you are going to see Me; because I live, you also will live. On that day you will know that I am in My Father, and you are in Me, and I in you. (John 14.16-20)

God is with us. The Father is in us and we are in Him. The Son is in us, and we are in Him. The Holy Spirit is in us, and we are in Him. The nearness of God to us transcends geography. We live in Him. He lives in us.

We have come to know and have believed the love which God has for us. God is love, and the one who remains in love remains in God, and God remains in him. (1 John 4.16)

For this reason I bend my knees before the Father, from whom every family in heaven and on earth derives its name, that He would grant you, according to the riches of His glory, to be strengthened with power through His Spirit in the inner self, so that Christ may dwell in your hearts through faith; and that you, being rooted and grounded in love, may be able to comprehend with all the saints what is the width and length and height and depth, and to know the love of Christ which surpasses knowledge, that you may be filled to all the fullness of God. (Ephesians 3.16-19)

Or do you not know that your body is a temple of the Holy Spirit within you, whom you have from God, and that you are not your own? (1 Corinthians 6.19)

And we know that the Son of God has come, and has given us understanding so that we may know Him who is true; and we are in Him who is true, in His Son Jesus Christ. This is the true God and eternal life. (1 John 5.20)

But it is due to Him that you are in Christ Jesus, who became to us wisdom from God, and righteousness and sanctification, and redemption, (1 Corinthians 1.30)

I have been crucified with Christ. It is no longer I who live, but Christ who lives in me. And the life I now live in the flesh I live by faith in the Son of God, who loved me and gave himself for me. (Galatians 2.20)

Therefore if anyone is in Christ, this person is a new creation; the old things passed away; behold, new things have come. (2 Corinthians 5.17)

So you too, consider yourselves to be dead to sin, but alive to God in Christ Jesus.

These are just a few of the hundreds of passages emphasizing the Person and Presence of God. The focus of our lives should not be that Jesus lived. It is that Jesus lives. He is alive, and He is with us. He is alive, and He is listening to the words I speak. He is alive, and He sees the things I do. God is here and He is active in my life. God is Present. Right now. God is here.

When we realize with every fiber of our being that we are in the Presence of God, it changes us. A great example of this is the story of Joseph. It is a familiar story. Joseph was the youngest son of Jacob and through no fault of his own, he was Jacob's favorite child. Jacob spoiled Joseph and as a result, his siblings hated him. One day they decided to kill him and threw him into a dry well. Perhaps they were going to let him die of thirst, or bury him alive. We don't know. They did not do it because they saw a slave trader going by and realized they could make some money. They sold their brother into slavery.

Let that sink in. It is important. Joseph has committed no crime. He has not sinned. He is innocent. He is a victim. His own family sold him to a slave trader and then faked his death to his father. The slave trader took Joseph to Egypt and sold him to a man named Potipher.

Notice something.

*"The **Lord was with Joseph**, so he became a successful man. And he was in the house of his master, the Egyptian. Now his master saw that **the Lord was with him**..." (Genesis 39:2-3a)*

How could this be possible? His brothers betrayed him. Slave traders bought and sold him. He is the property of an Egyptian royalty. God is with him. Others could see God was with him. This goes against what we think. We believe that if God is with us, then life will be great. If God is with us, we will not get sick. If God is with us, we advance at work and have financial freedom. We believe the lie that if God is with us, then great things happen to us.

The emphasis is not on how wonderful Joseph's live was. It is on the fact that even as a slave in a foreign land, Joseph could live in the Presence of God. Joseph differed from others. It was not his ability. It was the fact that he lived with the Person and Presence of God.

The story continues with Joseph becoming the head slave of the house. Potipher's wife want to have sex with Joseph and he refuses because it is a sin against God. Joseph knows God is with Him and the Presence of God determines his moral choices. The wife frames Joseph for attempted rape and they put him in Pharoah's dungeon.

Retrace the story. Joseph's brothers attacked him and sold him into slavery. He is the property of a foreign man in a foreign country. He refuses to sin against his God and as a result is put in the worse prison in the world. Now read what the Bible says happened to him.

But the **Lord was with Joseph** *and extended kindness to him, and gave him favor in the sight of the chief jailer...* **the Lord was with him***..." (Genesis 39:21,23)*

Joseph lived a life of betrayal after betrayal. He was innocent, attacked, sold, framed and imprisoned. God was with him. The reason Joseph could endure such hardship was the Person and Presence of God. Fast forward to the end of the story. Pharoah elevated Joseph to the second most powerful person in the world and as a result saves the lives of millions of people, including his family. He forgives them for all they did to him and restores them. How could he do this? It was because throughout his life, in the lowest valley and the highest mountain, he knew God was with him.

How would you react differently to adversity if you could actually see God standing beside you? How would you respond to the challenges of life if you knew God was with you?

The heart of discipleship is simply living in the Presence and Person of Jesus.

In June 2018, my wife and I received a phone call no one should ever have to answer. My 29-year-old son was in the hospital dying. I put our journey together in a little book, "How Can My Son Be Dead". The bottom line of this horrendous story is simple. The Presence and Person of Jesus is the only thing that gave us the strength to endure. God's Presence encourages us. His Presence strengthens us. In the months following Seth's death, people kept trying to teach us theology. My friends talked to us and mailed us books about God's Sovereignty. "God has a plan." People told us a million times. In all honesty, from the moment the phone rang until this sentence two years later, I did not need a Bible lesson. I need(ed) Jesus.

The heart of discipleship is simply living in the Presence and Person of Jesus.

ABIDE IN CHRIST

We live outside of the USA. In 2007, we moved to South America. For the past 14 years we have not been immersed in American culture or politics. We also limit our social media. This is why we were so shocked to see the huge divide in American Culture. We discovered during the Presidential election of 2016, and again in 2020, many of our Christian brothers and sisters appear to be influenced more by their political affiliation than Christ. I posted several times my amazement at the name calling, aggression and seeming hatred on social media by Christians. My wife and I talk often about this. How can people who we know are Christians and truly decent people, be so mean online and over opinions? We believe it is because of influence. We have allowed the constant bombardment of news and media to shape us. My source of news and current events seeks to portray the opposing side as evil. It does not matter if you are liberal or conservative. Both sides seek to gain ground by convincing us the other side is the enemy of America. The media, conservative and liberal, influence us.

At this very moment, who or what has the most influence on your next decision? Be honest. On a moment-by-moment basis, how much actual influence does the Eternal and Unbroken Presence of Jesus Christ have on your life? Does your social media presence agree with your answer?

I am not asking if you are in sin. This is not talking about making a moral choice or not. My question is, how much influence does the Presence of Jesus have in your life, on your life, this moment. I believe the answer is very little.

Our morality, politics, capitalism, religion, our tradition, family may have tremendous influence on us. The particular news channel or talk show we follow influences us. Our peer group and church influence us. All these things help shape us. They have formulated my worldview. My question is more pro-active.

How often during the day do you think of, listen to, or talk to Jesus?

We have an enemy. He truly wants to destroy us. However, he is wise. He is the Deceiver and the father of lies. God warns us to watch out for his traps.

But I am afraid that, as the serpent deceived Eve by his craftiness, your minds will be led astray from the simplicity and purity of devotion to Christ. For if one comes and preaches another Jesus whom we have not preached, or you receive a different spirit which you have not received, or a different gospel which you have not accepted, you bear this beautifully (2 Corinthians 11.3-4)

I am amazed that you are so quickly deserting Him who called you by the grace of Christ, for a different gospel; which is really not another; only there are some who are disturbing you and want to distort the gospel of Christ. But even if we, or an angel from heaven, should preach to you a gospel contrary to what we have preached to you, he is to be accursed! As we have said before, so I say again now, if any man is preaching to you a gospel contrary to what you received, he is to be accursed! (Galatians 1:6-9)

Satan deceived Eve through his craftiness. He talked her into believing something not true. God warns us that the same thing may happen to us. We will leave the simplicity of the gospel. Satan can lead us astray the same way he has deceived humanity since the garden of Eden.

In Galatians, people were preaching and teaching a gospel of Jesus and the Spirit. The problem is they were preaching a different gospel. They were preaching a gospel of works and conformity to outward rituals and rules. The people were listening to this false gospel, and they were being deceived by it.

The Lord's bond-servant must not be quarrelsome, but be kind to all, able to teach, patient when wronged, with gentleness correcting those who are in opposition, if perhaps God may grant them repentance leading to the knowledge of the truth, and they may come to their senses and escape from the snare of the devil, having been held captive by him to do his will. (2 Timothy 2:24-26)

Notice God's servant is to be full of fruit (kind, patient, gentleness) as they correct those in opposition to the truth. Why are these people in opposition? They are against God and need to repent because they have fallen to the snare of the devil and are being held captive by him. We are to guard ourselves from the snares, deceits and craftiness of Satan.

The Bible teaches us,

No wonder, for even Satan disguises himself as an angel of light. Therefore, it is not surprising if his servants also disguise themselves as servants of righteousness, whose end will be according to their deeds." (2 Corinthians 11.14-15)

We have not paid attention to this and as a result Satan has deceived us. If the devil cannot get us with evil, he will get us with good. He rarely tempts us to go murder, or to rob a bank, or become a prostitute or some other big evil type of sin. So, the devil just gets us to do what is not bad. As long as it keeps us from God's will for our lives. If doing something good keeps us from living in the will of God, then Satan will get us to do good. An outstanding example would be all the incredibly moral cults. They do good. They live nice and moral lives. They are heading to a Christless hell for eternity. The devil is deceiving them with good.

He has done the same thing in the church. He gets us to make a swap for what is God's will to do what is 'not bad'. Let me give you a few examples right off of the top of my head where good has replaced the best to the detriment of God's kingdom.

Tithing replaces generosity. We struggle to get people to donate money, not only to world evangelism but even to the church. This is because it is a rare thing to meet a generous person. It is not that rare to meet a tither, but generous people are few. We have made the high bar in our churches the tithe and no longer even aim for overflowing generosity, and therefore the kingdom and the world suffers.

Following the rules replaces following Christ. We just do what our religion teaches us and therefore have rules on everything from modesty to music. We do not teach our people how to listen to the Spirit and apply the Word to this moment of their lives. We do not preach freedom and allow them to be led by the Holy Spirit. We do not need to listen to the Spirit because the rule has already spoken. We have replaced the Law of the Old Testament with the Law of the Church. It is a good law. It is a moral law. It is not God's will.

Ministry in the church replaces serving our community. We only have a few hours of free time each week, and we use it within the walls of a church building instead of seeking to serve our neighbors. We do not motivate our people to open the doors of their home with gifts of hospitality. We do not seek to have them help the marginalized or disenfranchised of the culture. We do not get them to spend time in community service. Our goal is to have a volunteer in the nursery at church. That is a good thing, but do we really believe that God's desire for our cultural impact is to change diapers for 20 minutes a month?

The local church has replaced world evangelism and discipleship. We have become myopic and desire to build our local church in both attendance and structures. It is a fact that 98% of all the money given to a local church stays within gate doors of that church. Instead of preaching world missions, we talk about local missions. I believe part of this is because we can call anything we do local missions and not feel guilty about our lack of support for world evangelism. The vast majority of the need for evangelism is outside of our Sunday morning service. Yet, we refuse to reach out of that moment and into a world. Once more, you can see how a good thing, supporting the local church, has replaced the best thing, supporting the local church in its mission to evangelize and disciple the world.

Bible study replaces Bible application. We study out the wazoo, but never truly apply anything. Our sermons, classes, seminars, conferences, seminaries, and podcasts are all about learning more Bible. However, when was the last time that you left church a different person, behaving differently, and noticeably different to those around you? We aren't changing. We are just learning. We do not read the Bible, nor study the Scripture, to change our lives. We do it to know more about the Bible and Bible times.

Church attendance replaces Fellowship. The Bible teaches a community of believers who are actively engaged in serving and motivating each other. We shake hands for three minutes before the worship service begins and call it fellowship. Instead of being involved in each other's lives, we attend church with each other. In the best-case scenario, we may also go to a small group where we study, not apply, the Bible together. It is a far cry from the community God desires, but it is good enough for us (and Satan).

We have replaced differing from the culture with what we call holy. We have redefined the term holy to mean 'avoid the things our rules say avoid', yet we can be just like our lost neighbor. The Bible calls us to stand out in terms of how we live our lives and being holy means being set apart for God to use. In our lives, the only actual difference between us and the lost in our community is where we spend Sunday morning. We go to church and they go to the golf course. Other than that, we are pretty much equal in all we do. We are not doing horrible acts of violent sin, and neither is our neighbor.

We have allowed doctrinal assent to replace Spiritual fruit. I have already talked about this. In our current systems we can be mean, impatient, unkind, harsh, divisive, covetous, and angry, but if we can describe salvation by faith and defend predestination and discuss end-time theology, then we believe we are mature Christians. I have known some mean and divisive church leaders, pastors and elders. They look nothing like Jesus. They have no spiritual fruit. They agree with and can teach good theology, so we lift them up as leaders. We have replaced the fruit and character of Jesus with a nod of our head.

Now, the point of this chapter and I believe one of the most damaging deceptions and swaps we have made.

We have allowed a quiet time to replace our relationship with Jesus. Let me say that again. I think one of the most effect-ive tools Satan uses to keep us from having an effective relation-ship with Christ is a quiet time.

God wants us all the time, we give Him some time and feel wonderful about it. God wants us twenty-four hours a day to focus on and be dependent upon Him. We give Him a distracted 15 minutes in the morning and people consider us super Chris-tians. Our relationship with Jesus is just a little spice that we add to our lives, like sprinkling parmesan cheese on pasta. It is just a little flavor.

We have done a huge disservice to the church. We have taught people to acknowledge Jesus, then ignore Him, repeat the next day. I believe the reason we do not have a passion for the world, a passion for the poor, a passion for the lost or a passion for the local church is because we don't have a passion for Jesus. The reason that we don't have a passion for Jesus is it is difficult to have passion about something you only spend 10-15 minutes a day on.

Let's be honest, we spend more time on social media, news, television and sports than we do on Jesus. This is because our church culture taught us the Christian life is simply a list of things to do and things to avoid. We also make sure to pepper it with the big four: Read your Bible, Pray, go to Church and try to get other people to, etc. The Bible does not teach this at all. The heart of discipleship, and the Christian life, is knowing Jesus is with you right now. Look at what has become known as the Great Commission. It is the heart of our evangelism and discipleship.

Go therefore and make disciples of all the nations, baptizing them in the name of the Father and the Son and the Holy Spirit, teaching them to observe all that I commanded you; and lo, I am with you always, even to the end of the age. (Matthew 28:19-20)

We spend all of our energy on studying the Bible, the first part of the commission. How much time have you spent teaching, or have been taught, on applying the second? He will be with us, even to the end of the ages? The Bible teaches the Christian life is lived on a moment-by-moment basis as we depend on the Holy Spirit to keep us connected with Jesus. This is called yielding to Him. Yes, we are to teach and learn what the Bible says. However, we are also to learn how to live in light of the truth that the Author of the Bible we are learning, God Himself, is with us. He is with us in this moment.

One of the reasons that we should be sexually pure is because God is with us, even in the act of sex itself. He is there.

Marriage is to be held in honor among all, and the marriage bed is to be undefiled; for fornicators and adulterers God will judge. Make sure that your character is free from the love of money, being content with what you have; for He Himself has said, 'I will never desert you, nor will I ever forsake you,' so that we confidently say, "The Lord is my helper, I will not be afraid. What will man do to me?" (Hebrews 13:4-6)

Or do you not know that your body is a temple of the Holy Spirit who is in you, whom you have from God, and that you are not your own? (1 Corinthians 6:19)

It is the presence of God with us that allows us to maintain our moral purity and keep a right focus on the physical world in our possession and our relationships. He is with me. He will help me. He will never leave me. My body is actually the Temple where He lives. He is here in this moment during this activity. He is present.

This is not just some theory. It is practically living out the presence of Christ. It is depending on Him and the Holy Spirit to conform you to His Image. It is what the Bible is talking about all of those times it uses words like 'Abide', 'Live in', and 'Walk'. It means moment by moment depending upon Him. These verses are teaching us our Christian life is not determined by a one-time agreement with the truth that Christ died for our sins. Our initial confession and faith in Him forgive us and gives us eternal life. However, the true life of the Christian is a moment-by-moment dependence upon the Holy Spirit. It is in this breath, with this heartbeat, in this thought, with these words letting the Holy Spirit guide me and Christ fill me. The church teaching of giving Jesus a 15-minute devotion before you start your day is NOT in the Bible.

Look at just some verses that teach us to live in the moment in Christ. There are two ways God teaches this. The first is by the word 'Abide'. This phrase means to live in, to be connected to. It means your life is defined by this connection. The other word is the word 'Walk'. This phrase describes the moment-by-moment connection living the Christian life has with the Father. This connection defines every step you take. Read the following verses. Do they teach a quiet time, or an 'all-the-time'?

Abide in Me, and I in you. As the branch cannot bear fruit of itself unless it abides in the vine, so neither can you unless you abide in Me. (John 15:4)

I am the vine, you are the branches; he who abides in Me and I in him, he bears much fruit, for apart from Me you can do nothing. (John 15:5)

If you abide in Me, and My words abide in you, ask whatever you wish, and it will be done for you. (John 15:7)

Just as the Father has loved Me, I have also loved you; abide in My love. (John 15:9)

If you keep My commandments, you will abide in My love; just as I have kept My Father's commandments and abide in His love. (John

15:10)

Therefore we have been buried with Him through baptism into death, so that as Christ was raised from the dead through the glory of the Father, so we too might walk in newness of life. (Romans 6:4)

For we walk by faith, not by sight (2 Corinthians 5:7)

But I say, walk by the Spirit, and you will not carry out the desire of the flesh. (Galatians 5:16)

If we live by the Spirit, let us also walk by the Spirit. (Galatians 5:25)

Therefore I, the prisoner of the Lord, implore you to walk in a manner worthy of the calling with which you have been called, (Ephesians 4:1)

and walk in love, just as Christ also loved you and gave Himself up for us, an offering and a sacrifice to God as a fragrant aroma. (Ephesians 5:2)

for you were formerly darkness, but now you are Light in the Lord; walk as children of Light. (Ephesians 5:8)

Therefore as you have received Christ Jesus the Lord, so walk in Him, (Colossians 2:6)

but if we walk in the Light as He Himself is in the Light, we have fellowship with one another, and the blood of Jesus His Son cleanses us from all sin. (1 John 1:7)

These verses show we are to live in Him. He is to live in us. His life in us is what gives us life. It is as we abide in Him and He abides in us we receive the ability to glorify Him, bear fruit for Him, and do the work He has called us to do. It comes from LIVING, ABIDING, REMAINING in Him. Each step I take is to be in step with Who He Is and the fact I am in Him and He is in me.

Bill had a terrible day at work. Nothing major, just things did not go as he planned. He was slightly grumpy when he left the office. As he pulled up to his house, he saw the kid's toys scattered in the yard and driveway and it was the final straw. He walked into the house, and his first words were angry and corrective.

Sandy, his wife, has four kids. Two are in elementary school, one is a preschooler and the other a nursing baby. She feels frustrated because it seems like her entire vocabulary has been reduced to single syllables and no matter what she does, she cannot keep up with the destruction the children bring to the house. She feels overwhelmed, inadequate and unappreciated. When Bill came in the house, even though he was complaining about the kids, both Bill and Sandy knew he was really griping at her failure as a mother. She retaliated by defending the children and pointing out something that Bill had said he would do (fix the toy box) but had not yet done, therefore placing the fault on him.

Thus, begins another of their peaceful fights. The words never go farther than what was just described, but the hurt, anger, frustration, and negative feelings were there for the rest of the evening. That night Bill wanted to have sex, but Sandy was too tired. Bill knew the actual reason was he upset her, but he rolled over and after about 10 minutes of sexual frustration and wrong thinking, fell asleep.

This is normal for Bill and Sandy. They have minor spats almost every day. The thing about this is Bill is not just a good Christian guy, he is an elder in the church. Bill and Sandy are role models of a Christian marriage. Their smiles and well-dressed children are examples for everyone each Sunday morning. They co-teach the church marriage conference every year on the couple's retreat.

However, I have a question. Where is Jesus in all of this? Is Jesus nothing more than a doctrine we believe or is He actually present in our lives? We say the latter but live like it is the former.

Let's look at another way that this could have played out...

Bill has had a terrible day at work. On the way home, he is thinking about the Lord and he realizes his attitude is revealing he needs Jesus. He senses his fruit is not honoring Christ. So he prays, "Lord Jesus, I sense anger inside of me over how the day went. It reveals to me I need you. You died because I am the type of man who would be angry and then take it out on my family. Will you forgive me, fill me with your Holy Spirit, and allow me to minster grace to my family when I arrive home?"

He pulls into the driveway and sees the toys. Once more, God is using the failures of others to reveal to Bill he needs repentance and faith in Christ. Bill prays, "Lord, I am still in need of you. I see these toys, and it makes me upset. That is not true. I am upset and the toys reveal it. Lord, I need to teach my kids to respect their toys and my rules, but I know now is not the time because my heart is not clean. You said when we see a brother overtaken in a fault, we need to be spiritual before addressing them. I am not ready to speak to them in a spirit of meekness. I forgive my children. Will you forgive me for my heart of anger, fill me with your Spirit and allow me to bless my family with love?"

What do you think would happen when Bill walks in the house if this is his attitude and response all the time?

Bill fails. So, let's say this time it is Sandy who sees her heart and responds correctly. Bill walks in the house upset. The first words out of his mouth that Sandy hears are words of anger. He speaks words of hostility towards the kids, and Sandy feels like it is a judgement of her. Instead of focusing on Bill and his words, she turns to the Christ she knows is Present and prays, "Lord Jesus, I need you. As Bill is speaking, I feel judged and I feel like defending myself. I want to put him in his place and make him see how good I am. I want him to know he could not do it either, and he is treating us sinfully. My heart is to respond in anger. At this moment I see anger, frustration and malice in my life. Lord, you died because I am the type of wife who would defend and attack. You died because I am the type of woman who wants to prove my worth to others instead of finding my identity in you. Right now I can hear and see my husband needs to be loved unconditionally. I don't want to love him in that manner. My lack of love is not because of him. My heart is the problem. Lord, will you forgive me of my sins such as my anger, my lack of faith in You working and my desire to attack? Will You forgive me, fill me with Your Holy Spirit, and allow me to share Your love with my husband in his time of need?"

What do you think would happen if that was her response?

Denise and I have been married for over 36 years. We discovered this truth of abiding in Christ and testing, confessing, and repenting on a moment-by-moment basis shortly after our marriage. Because of this, in over 36 years of marriage, we have only had a handful (we can only remember two) of sinful arguments. A sinful argument is where both people are speaking, acting, thinking and doing sinful things. We have had plenty of disagreements. However, we discuss the disagreements in a manner that promotes growth and understanding. I want to emphasize this truth.

Three years ago, our family was all together at Christmas time. Our family comprises 11 children and three in-laws. We live on two continents and in three states. Our entire family does not get together often. The four younger kids had gone to bed. The older seven sat in the living room and chatted. Denise and I were listening to them talk to each other about growing up in our home and what it was like to be a Holman. As they were talking about the constant love in our home, I interjected a question. I asked them to be honest with me. I assured them I wanted to hear their perspective and know their hearts.

I said, "How many times can you guys remember seeing, hearing, or even knowing mom and I were angry at each other and having an argument?" Their answer was never. Not one time could they remember this happening. I pressed the issue. They all agreed. None of them remembered an argument.

I followed up with this question: "How many times do you guys remember mom or me being angry and expressing anger sinfully towards you?" They could remember once from me and once from Denise, not the same time I might add.

I believe them. This is not because we are super Christians

or have the perfect marriage. It is because God has taught us to abide in Him. Our goal is to please Him, not at the judgement seat, but in this chair right now. We have learned, by the grace of God, He is Present, and we need Him. The reason our marriage is so wonderful is that God is incredible. He works so we confess, repent and reconcile constantly. Jesus did not die so we could miss hell. He died in order for us to be like HIM.

We may be two Christians who are married, but our marriages will only reflect CHRIST if He is the actual center of every moment.

How much influence, on a moment-by-moment basis, does Jesus Christ have on your life? Is He the centerpiece of your life? Do you abide in Him? Do you depend upon Him? Do you listen to Him? Do you respond to Him? Is He the one in control of your thoughts, actions and words?

HOLY SPIRIT

In the mid 90s, I had the joy of working with three other Southern Baptist preachers on a school for church planters. We were deciding the scope and sequence. The school met for two hours twice a month on Saturdays for a total of 9 months. That meant we had only 36 hours to teach these church planters and laymen all they needed to know about basic theology, understanding culture, preaching, logistics, visioneering, leadership and legal requirements. We had the almost insurmountable task of choosing the most relevant things. I met with these other pastors for probably six weeks as we designed the courses and worked on the structure. Later on, we would share the teaching. For now, we had to decide on what needed to be taught. We were talking and one pastor pointed out that our theology had to include an understanding and an overview of God. It is called 'Theo-logy' after all. He volunteered to do a one-hour overview of the Father. A second pastor said he would teach for an hour on the Son. I said, "I will do the session on the Holy Spirit." What happened next shocked me. Two of the leadership team did not think we needed to take precious time on the Holy Spirit. One pointed out that we would not have Pentecostal or Charismatic church planters. The other said, "People already understand the Holy Spirit." I persisted and with the help of the third pastor was able to teach an hour on the Third Person of the Trinity.

I think there are three basic types of churches. There are churches which focus on God the Father and emphasize reformed doctrine. A second type focuses on God the Son and preach evangelistic messages. The final type concentrates on

God the Spirit, but in my opinion, they focus more on Spiritual Gifts than God Himself. We claim to be Trinitarians. In most cases, the evangelical church tends to ignore the Third Person of the Trinity.

I am concentrating on practical theology. Therefore, I will not seek to teach in depth on the Holy Spirit, just as I am not writing a theology on the Father or the Son. I do want us to know the Holy Spirit is the key to living a life that glorifies the Father. The Holy Spirit is the means of receiving God's power and accomplishing His purposes. Most importantly, the Holy Spirit lives inside of you and keeps you always in His Presence. The ignored truth of living the Christian life is so simple. It is remembering the Holy Spirit is with You and responding to His voice.

Look at these essential verses on the ministry of the Holy Spirit to the child of God.

I will ask the Father, and He will give you another Helper, so that He may be with you forever. (John 14.16)

But the Helper, the Holy Spirit whom the Father will send in My name, He will teach you all things, and remind you of all that I said to you. (John 14.26)

When the Helper comes, whom I will send to you from the Father, namely, the Spirit of truth who comes from the Father, He will testify about Me, (John 15.26)

but you will receive power when the Holy Spirit has come upon you; and you shall be My witnesses both in Jerusalem and in all Judea, and Samaria, and as far as the remotest part of the earth. (Acts 1.8)

And when they had prayed, the place where they had gathered together was shaken, and they were all filled with the Holy Spirit and began to speak the word of God with boldness. (Acts 4.31)

So the church throughout Judea, Galilee, and Samaria enjoyed peace, as it was being built up; and as it continued in the fear of the Lord and in the comfort of the Holy Spirit, it kept increasing. (Acts 9.31)

so that the requirement of the Law might be fulfilled in us who do not walk according to the flesh but according to the Spirit. For those who are in accord with the flesh set their minds on the things of the flesh, but those who are in accord with the Spirit, the things of the Spirit. For the mind set on the flesh is death, but the mind set on the Spirit is life and peace, because the mind set on the flesh is hostile toward God; for it does not subject itself to the law of God, for it is not even able to do so, and those who are in the flesh cannot please God. However, you are not in the flesh but in the Spirit, if indeed the Spirit of God dwells in you. But if anyone does not have the Spirit of Christ, he does not belong to Him. If Christ is in you, though the body is dead because of sin, yet the spirit is alive because of righteousness. But if the Spirit of Him who raised Jesus from the dead dwells in you, He who raised Christ Jesus from the dead will also give life to your mortal bodies through His Spirit who dwells in you. So then, brothers and sisters, we are under obligation, not to the flesh, to live according to the flesh—for if you are living in accord with the flesh, you are going to die; but if by the Spirit you are putting to death the deeds of the body, you will live. For all who are being led by the Spirit of God, these are sons and daughters of God. For you have not received a spirit of slavery leading to fear again, but you have received a spirit of adoption as sons and daughters by which we cry out, "Abba! Father!" The Spirit Himself testifies with our spirit that we are children of God, (Romans 8.4-16)

Now in the same way the Spirit also helps our weakness; for we do not know what to pray for as we should, but the Spirit Himself intercedes for us with groanings too deep for words; and He who searches the hearts knows what the mind of the Spirit is, because He intercedes for the saints according to the will of God. (Romans 8.26-27)

for the kingdom of God is not eating and drinking, but righteousness and peace and joy in the Holy Spirit. (Romans 14.17)

Now may the God of hope fill you with all joy and peace in believing, so that you will abound in hope by the power of the Holy Spirit. (Romans 15:13)

But I say, walk by the Spirit, and you will not carry out the desire of the flesh. For the desire of the flesh is against the Spirit, and the Spirit against the flesh; for these are in opposition to one another, in order to keep you from doing whatever you want. But if you are led by the Spirit, you are not under the Law. Now the deeds of the flesh are evident, which are: sexual immorality, impurity, indecent behavior, idolatry, witchcraft, hostilities, strife, jealousy, outbursts of anger, selfish ambition, dissensions, factions, envy, drunkenness, carousing, and things like these, of which I forewarn you, just as I have forewarned you, that those who practice such things will not inherit the kingdom of God. But the fruit of the Spirit is love, joy, peace, patience, kindness, goodness, faithfulness, gentleness, self-control; against such things there is no law. Now those who belong to Christ Jesus crucified the flesh with its passions and desires. If we live by the Spirit, let's follow the Spirit as well. (Galatians 5:16-25)

And do not get drunk with wine, in which there is debauchery, but be filled with the Spirit, (Ephesians 5.18)

For who among people knows the thoughts of a person except the spirit of the person that is in him? So also the thoughts of God no one knows, except the Spirit of God. (1 Corinthians 2.11)

Do you not know that you are a temple of God and that the Spirit of God dwells in you? (1 Corinthians 3.16)

Or do you not know that your body is a temple of the Holy Spirit within you, whom you have from God, and that you are not your own? (1 Corinthians 6.19)

Here is a good question for you. After reading the above verses and seeing the importance of the Holy Spirit to the Christian life, how much emphasis do you place on your relationship with Him? Most of the churches I tend to line up with doctrinally, Bible and Baptistic ones, relegate the ministry of the

Holy Spirit mainly to the past. We act like His job ended when He finished writing the Bible. Now, the Holy Spirit will convict people of their need for Jesus. After that, we ignore the Holy Spirit in our lives.

This is one of the reasons the church, and discipleship, is weak. The mark of a Christian is to be led of the Holy Spirit (Romans 8.14). The method of overcoming sin in our lives is to walk in the Spirit (Galatians 5.16). We must retrain ourselves. We were taught discipleship was behavior modification. This leads to legalism. I taught a series against legalism in one of the churches I pastored. In the series, I said teaching the truth about grace could often result in an accusation of heresy. The reason is we do not live under the law of Moses. We do not live under man made laws and traditions. As a believer, I am saved, period. I taught we do not have to read our Bibles. We do not have to pray. We do not have to attend church. We do not have to share Christ. We do not have to give money. The reason we do not have to do those things is wonderful. In Christ, we want to do them. This was in one sermon. The next week would pick up on these points and speak of the transforming power of the Holy Spirit. Before the next week arrived, I had a man in our church tell me he was leaving because I was preaching heretical doctrine. He said, actually he yelled, our being under grace did not give us license to sin. Here is how I responded to him.

"Scott (not his real name), you are making a decision before hearing the full teaching. However, let me ask you something."

"I don't need to wait. This morning was heresy."

"Okay but let me ask you something." I continued. "Suppose you have two people who give their lives to Christ in our college ministry. They share a common background of typical lostness and sin. One of these two is assimilated into a solid Baptist church. He learns not to drink. He stops attending movies with an R rating. He changes his language and eliminates cussing. He is transformed into a good person who follows all of the rules found in Baptist culture. He doesn't do the "No-No's" and does do the "Good List". He attends church, reads his Bible and is in a small group."

"That is not legalism. That is spiritual growth." He said.

"Right. Now, the second fellow is different. He goes to our church. I meet with him and teach him about the Presence of God. He learns how to be filled with the Holy Spirit. He fine tunes his heart so he can hear the soft whisper of God and be led by the Spirit. He walks in the Spirit, which causes him to avoid the things of the flesh. His spends his entire waking day acknowledging the Presence of God and seeking to bring glory to Him. Which of these two men do you feel is more like Christ? Do you think it is the one who learned how to be a Baptist or the one who learned how to listen to the Holy Spirit? Do you think our rules and restrictions will result in someone become holier than a person being led by God?"

"I see what you are trying to say. That does not change the truth. We have things we have to do and things we cannot do. Your teaching heresy." He replied.

"Scott, I did not say we could do anything. There are things we cannot do. Doing them will not make us lose our salvation. Not doing them does not make us holy. We do not do them because we are living in the Presence and Power of God. He leads us. He fills us. He guides us. We avoid sin and pursue righteousness because of His Presence and Power. My point is we do not have to read our Bible. We want to read it. We do not have to go to church. We want to go to church. We do not have to give generously. We want to give generously. We do not live under laws. God's grace and the power of the Holy Spirit lead us to exceed our own codes of morality. The Holy Spirit inside of us leads us into the will of God."

He and his family left the church. He could not comprehend this truth. The Holy Spirit will transform us into the image of the Son. There appear to be two avenues. The first and most widely traveled road is to follow our rules and become like each other. We can become Playdough Christians who are molded into the image of our peer group. The road less traveled follows the Holy Spirit. This path leads us to a destination of Christlikeness. I know there is a huge overlap. Our own systems mimic the righteous life the Holy Spirit leads us to live. A true believer who is assimilated into a Bible teaching church will lead a life of morality. The difference is one of heart. We need to do these things in response to His leadership and not in an effort to gain His approval.

The Holy Spirit transforms every relationship as we allow ourselves to be filled with Him. In Ephesians 5, God tells us to be filled with the Holy Spirit. I will put the verses in context below. This phrase does not mean we get more of the Holy Spirit. He is a Person and He is God. We have all of the Holy Spirit. It means that He gets more of us. He controls our attitudes, thoughts, and actions. He takes over our relationships. It is God's will for the Holy Spirit to control us in every area. The example is a drunk person. If someone is drunk, the alcohol controls all of them. We are not to be drunk. We are to be filled, controlled by, the Holy Spirit. As you read the passage below, notice that once we are filled with the Holy Spirit, every area of our life will show it. We will change how we speak to God. We treat other believers with love and kindness. Our marriages reflect the love of Christ and the church. Our parenting points our children to Jesus. Our work relationships are submitted to the kingdom of God. You cannot be a disciple of Christ and not be Spirit-Filled.

Therefore do not be foolish, but understand what the will of the Lord is. And do not get drunk with wine, in which there is debauchery, but be filled with the Spirit, speaking to one another in psalms and hymns and spiritual songs, singing and making melody with your hearts to the Lord; always giving thanks for all things in the name of our Lord Jesus Christ to our God and Father; and subject yourselves to one another in the fear of Christ. Wives, subject yourselves to your own husbands, as to the Lord. For the husband is the head of the wife, as Christ also is the head of the church, He Himself being the Savior of the body. But as the church is subject to Christ, so also the wives ought to be to their husbands in everything. Husbands, love your wives, just as Christ also loved the church and gave Himself up for her, so that He might sanctify her, having cleansed her by the washing of water with the word, that He might present to Himself the church in all her glory, having no spot or wrinkle or any such thing; but that she would be holy and blameless. So husbands also ought to love their own wives as their own bodies. He who loves his own wife loves himself; for no one ever hated his own flesh, but nourishes and cherishes it, just as Christ also does the church, because we are parts of His body. For this reason a man shall leave his father and his mother and be joined to his wife, and the two shall become one flesh. This mystery is great; but I am speaking with reference to Christ and the church. Nevertheless, as for you individually, each husband is to love his own wife the same as himself, and the wife must see to it that she respects her husband. Children, obey your parents in the Lord, for this is right. Honor your father and mother (which is the first commandment with a promise), so that it may turn out well for you, and that you may live long on the earth. Fathers, do not provoke your children to anger, but bring them up in the discipline and instruction of the Lord. Slaves, be obedient to those who are your masters according to the flesh, with fear and trembling, in the sincerity of your heart, as to Christ; not by way of eye-service, as people-pleasers, but as slaves of Christ, doing the will of God from the heart. With good-will render service, as to the Lord, and not to people, knowing that whatever good thing each one does, he will receive this back from the Lord, whether slave or free. And masters, do the same things to them, and give up threatening, knowing that both their Master and yours is in heaven, and there is no partiality with Him. (Ephesians 5.17-6.9)

We follow Christ in the context of human relationships. The Holy Spirit controls our attitudes and actions. He tells me how to respond to my life. This is the heart of discipleship. It is given other terms. We call it walking or being led by the Spirit. The bottom line is that you cannot live the Christian life unless you live in dependence upon the Person and Presence of the Holy Spirit.

SPIRITUAL FRUIT

When I was young, my parents had a sizeable garden. At one point it was almost a half of an acre in size. We grew our own vegetables and fruits. That garden has been a source of near bitterness for me and my siblings. My parents made us prepare the soil. We had to make the rows by hand with a hoe. We planted the seeds and watered and weeded it until the crops grew. I spent hours in the garden with a water hose in my hand. I worked for hours in the garden picking weeds. I worked in the Texas heat. I hated that garden. My parents would brag to others about how good 'their' garden had been and how much they had received from it. That change in pronouns used to make me so upset. The fact they took credit for my garden is irrelevant. It is just my first opportunity to complain in print. My point is I could instantly tell you what type of plant a certain fruit came from. If you held up a watermelon, I knew what type of vine it had grown on. If you showed me a strawberry, even before the invention of the internet I could tell you the name of the plant that had it had grown on. I could do this for every single fruit. I still can perform this amazing feat of horticulture. What is my secret? It is simple. I could name the fruit plant by the fruit. A watermelon grows on a watermelon vine. A strawberry bush produces strawberries. An orange is most definitely from an orange tree. The fruit reveals the tree, and the tree determines the fruit.

This is important. This is another life-changing truth. I came across this over 20 years ago. I was studying spiritual fruit, and something happened. I realized how central fruit is to the Christian life. I took time and looked at every verse in the Bible which mentioned the word fruit. I looked at every passage that mentioned 'a' fruit. I read every single place God used the word love. I did the same thing for all the other listed fruits. I took a pink highlighter and went through my study Bible and every time God mentioned a spiritual fruit, I marked it. The amount of pink highlighter surprised me. I studied the purpose of fruit.

In the Bible, fruit does three things, and those same three things happen in our lives today. Fruit reveals to us the tree it came from. Fruit reproduces life. It also gives nourishment to others. This is the same thing that Spiritual Fruit does in our lives. We can see the truth about who we are by the fruit our lives manifest. Our lives are to bring other people into the Kingdom and spur them towards maturity. This describes the reproduction of fruit. The final thing is that we are to be a blessing to other people. These are the purposes of fruit.

I discovered fruit is the standard by which God measures our growth. We like to use other things. We use things such as church attendance, quiet times, Bible reading, doctrinal knowledge and/or the use of our spiritual gifts. We evaluate our lives by how much we read the Bible, pray, go to church and try to get other people to read their Bibles, pray and go to church. We like to use these things because they are safe, and we have control over them. If good doctrine is how I am evaluated and how I evaluate others, I can study and read. If church attendance is the standard, I can go to church. If morality is what we are looking for, then I can make sure my life looks good on the outside.

Fruit is not like that. Fruit is not something we control, it is something that God does in us, and it is what God uses to determine whether we are growing in Him. As I taught in the section on love, I cannot love others unconditionally. I am incapable of this feat. Therefore, if unconditional love is the evaluator of my life, I will either be a failure, or I must depend on God to help me. Fruit is what God measures us by because fruit reveals who we really are and how much we are abiding in Him.

I looked up the fruits individually, and then the word fruit itself in the Bible. For example, God uses the word love 880 times and the word goodness 802 times. The Bible uses the word fruit, and the actual fruits of the Holy Spirit, 4,499 times. A quiet time is never mentioned in the Bible. The Bible doesn't tell us to read a few verses and then pray for five minutes every morning. However, God uses the word fruit 4,499 times. This is serious to God! If fruit is so vital to the Christian life, we need to understand what it is.

Fruit is who we really are. I can try to deceive you and myself by acting like someone else, but my fruit reveals the truth. In the story I told in the previous chapter, I was pretending to be a good Christian pastor and father. My son could see by my fruit of anger and hostility that I was not who I was pretending to be.

It is by my fruit that I can know myself. We love to emphasize in our culture that we should not judge other people. I am not saying you can judge me, although you can, according to the Bible. I can judge myself. I may think I am a great Christian man. My fruit reveals the truth.

You will know them by their fruits. Grapes are not gathered from thorn bushes nor figs from thistles, are they? So every good tree bears good fruit, but the bad tree bears bad fruit. A good tree cannot produce bad fruit, nor can a bad tree produce good fruit. Every tree that does not bear good fruit is cut down and thrown into the fire. So then, you will know them by their fruits." (Matthew. 7.16-20)

I love to illustrate this when I am teaching it by embarrassing a teenager. Here is what I do. While preaching, I pretend that my voice is a little strained. I find a teenager in the crowd and point to my water glass that I left on the front row. I ask them to bring it to me. As they hand it to me, I drop it so it spills all over the floor, on the stage, in front of everyone. This happens with a lot of smiling and laughter:

Joe: Oh my goodness! Look at that! Dude! Why is there water on the floor?
Teen: Because you dropped the cup?
Joe: No, that is not why. Also, you dropped the cup, don't

blame me. Why is there water on the floor?

Teen: Because it spilled.

Joe: No. Why is there water on the floor?

This continues to the frustration of the teenager until I stop and say, "There is water on the floor because there was water in the cup. If there would have been coffee in the cup, then there would be coffee on the floor. If there would have been juice in the cup, then there would be juice on the floor. There is water on the floor because there was water in the cup. What is in you is what comes out when you are bumped."

As the teen sits down to the grateful applause of the audience, I continue to point this truth out and apply it to our lives. We love to focus on the outside and make our cups appear good. However, what spills out when we are bumped is what was inside all the time.

At this point, I hold up my Bible. Unknown to the listeners, I have a tube of opened toothpaste inside of it. I show them the Bible and talk about how nice it is, the leather cover, and that it is God's word. This is our lives. We seek to appear good, and we contain (know) God's word. But what happens when our children disobey? What happens when a driver cuts us off in traffic? What happens when a co-worker does not deliver on their responsibility? What happens when my spouse is mean to me? What happens when the opposing political party member does something that I disagree with? What happens when life squeezes me? I squeeze the Bible, and to their surprise a long gooey stream of toothpaste oozed out of it. Every time that I have done this, there has been an audible expression of grossness such as "Uuugggh".

I ask them what it is and pretty quickly someone identifies toothpaste. Now, no one knew that it was inside the Bible. It was not until the Bible was squeezed that what was hidden inside became visible for all of us to see.

That is how Spiritual fruit works. My fruit is the knee-jerk reaction that I have to life. It is what falls from my branches when I am bumped. It is not the pretty decorated mug that I carry around. It is what spills out of that beautiful mug when I drop it. At this point, I put three identical cups on a table. One cup is full of water. The other cup is full of coffee. The last cup has orange juice. I ask them which cup has which liquid. We talk about it some and then even vote. I hold up one cup and then pretend to get bumped by someone and I spill some contents.

As soon as that happens, I then ask again, "What is inside of this cup?" Everyone knows the answer because they saw the contents of the cup when I was bumped, and they spilled out. I repeat this with all three cups. I then finish by putting the cups on the table but hiding the order. I ask again, "Based on appearance, what is in this cup?" No one knows since they all look identical. It is not until they are bumped and the liquid spills out that we can know what was inside.

When something bumps me, the thing that comes out is what was inside. I can know my life and my walk with Christ by what comes out when I am bumped. It may not be visible to others, but I can see it. It is my knee-jerk reaction. It may not be what I do, it is what I want to do. For example, a wife is snippy to her husband. His internal and immediate reaction is that he wants to put her in her place. He wants to be argumentative in return. He wants to one-up her comment with a great retort and put down. However, he has learned that if he does this, the marital spat is not worth the pleasure of the remark and he probably won't have sex tonight. So, he does not do it. He either says nothing or says something to try to smooth over the situation.

The fact that he WANTED to is what reveals his heart. He was not kind to his wife. He was selfish. He did not put her down because he is like Jesus. He chose to not argue because he wants to have sex. His fruit, that only he saw, is anger, malice, and selfishness. Other people saw a conflict diffused by a patient man. It was all an act. It was a conflict avoided by a selfish man who did not want to endure the consequences of revealing his heart to others.

Fruit reveals who I am. The reason that I am a grumpy and gripey person at home and not one at work is not because my wife and children are worse than my co-workers to be around. It is because I have learned I can be mean at home without real retaliation. I change my behavior and hide my character at work. At home, I allow my fruit to reveal who I am. I am a grumpy and mean person.

My children were in the kitchen one day, and one kid accidentally hurt another one by stepping on their bare toe. The hurt child, an eight-year-old, yelled in anger at their sibling and tried to push them.

I intervened and asked, "Why did you yell at your brother?"

My son responded, "He stepped on my toe."

"Yes", I said, "He stepped on your toe. But why did you yell at him?".

My son thought for a moment and said, "I yelled at him because in my heart there is anger, and when he stepped on my toe, it came out."

I told him he was correct, and it was why he needed the grace of God. He was the type of person who would yell and violently respond to a slight pain caused accidentally by his brother. He needed the gospel to become better than that. There was no punishment. My purpose was not to change his behavior, so he learned to muffle his angry response. My goal was to help him take that angry response to the cross and have Jesus exchange it for patience.

Can you see how incredibly profound this truth is, and can you imagine how much life would change if we would live it out? This little eight-year-old child already knew that the only way for anger to come out of him was if anger was in him. Nothing actually makes me angry. However, there are many things God can use to reveal the anger of my heart. Fruit reveals who we are to ourselves and to others, but let's focus on ourselves.

I came home and my wife had a horrible day. We have 11 children, and my wife is a homeschooling mother. This means her life is consumed with the trials of full time parenting multiple age kids. So, I came home, and she had a trying day. A short time after I am home, she speaks unkindly to me. Instantly I think to myself, "You cannot treat me that way. I have done nothing wrong. It is not my fault you don't make the kids obey, nor that the house is dirty. That is on you. You don't speak to me like that. I am your husband. I...."

The Holy Spirit convicts me. I realize what has happened. My wife bumped my branches and judgment, hostility, self-righteousness, and anger fell from the tree. So, I pray, "Dear Lord, I need You right now. I just realized that my heart is in sin. The things I wanted to say to Denise are not from your lips. Jesus, You died for me because I am the type of man who would be mean to a woman who has sacrificed all of her own desires for the good of my family and love of me. I see my fruit, and it is not pretty. Would you forgive me, fill me with your Spirit, and allow me to speak love to my wife?"

My fruit revealed to me my need for Jesus. I responded to it and He answered my prayer, allowing me to be gracious and loving to my wife. This is how fruit reveals who we truly are to us. Many times, probably over 100 in the years we have been in ministry, people have complimented my wife on how patient and kind she is. They have said that they can see it in how she treats the children, me and others. I had the children make a film for Mother's Day this year and in it they complimented her. Three of them mentioned how patient and gentle she is with them. Denise doesn't even know it. She doesn't try to be patient. She has not taken a life development course on kindness. It is the fruit of the Holy Spirit in her life. When she is bumped, patience, kindness and gentleness fall from the branches. She is this because of God.

Fruit reveals who we are to ourselves. It is also a measure of personal character growth. This is self-explanatory, but if I am angry when bumped, but over time in which I constantly repent and seek forgiveness I see that I am gentle when bumped, I know that I have grown a little more like Jesus.

But the fruit of the Spirit is love, joy, peace, patience, kindness, goodness, faithfulness, gentleness, self-control; against such things there is no law. (Galatians 5.22-23)

Now for this very reason also, applying all diligence, in your faith supply moral excellence, and in your moral excellence, knowledge, and in your knowledge, self-control, and in your self-control, perseverance, and in your perseverance, godliness, and in your godliness, brotherly kindness, and in your brotherly kindness, love. For if these qualities are yours and are increasing, they render you neither useless nor unfruitful in the true knowledge of our Lord Jesus Christ. (2 Peter 1.5-8)

Notice in 2 Peter that as God describes our growth, it is almost all fruit. I believe these, even knowledge is the fruit of the Holy Spirit because the knowledge that this is speaking of is the knowledge of God based upon context. Even if it is not, self-control, perseverance, kindness and love are mentioned. Then God's desire that we will not be 'unfruitful'. This goes back to the beginning of this chapter where I pointed out that we love to measure our spiritual growth by other metrics. Instead of evaluating my life by gentleness, peace and goodness, I like to point out that I can defend my particular view of election. I know my eschatology and I have a firm opinion on women in ministry. We have made our growth standard to be an increase in academic knowledge. How much do we know? It is amazing how we so many times our standard or focus has become the opposite of what the Bible teaches. Read the last part of 1 Corinthians 8:1, Knowledge makes arrogant, but love edifies. We focus on what we know and because of that we become arrogant. God says that love is the key, not knowledge, love, which is a fruit of the Holy Spirit. The Bible says that it is not our knowledge or actions that reveal our heart. It is our fruit.

We also see spiritual fruit in our evangelistic endeavors. It is not only in the physical world we see that the purpose of fruit is to reproduce the life of the tree, but the Bible also alludes to it in the spiritual world. If you do not have spiritual offspring, you really do not have fruit. Notice how Proverbs connects fruit with winning souls.

The fruit of the righteous is a tree of life, And he who is wise wins souls. (Proverbs 11.30)

Paul and John would refer to those that they helped come to know Christ and/or discipled as their 'children'.

To Timothy, my true child in the faith: Grace, mercy and peace from God the Father and Christ Jesus our Lord. (1 Timothy 1.2)

I have no greater joy than this, to hear of my children walking in the truth. (3 John 1.4)

Finally, we see in the Bible that bearing fruit is the expressed will of God for our lives.

My Father is glorified by this, that you bear much fruit, and so prove to be My disciples. (John. 15.8)

You did not choose Me but I chose you, and appointed you that you would go and bear fruit, and that your fruit would remain, so that whatever you ask of the Father in My name He may give to you. (John 15.16)

I mentioned in an earlier part that the metric of our lives is to glorify God. Here is an activity that I have done several times with pastors. I ask them what is the purpose of our ministry and our lives? I then gently lead them to the answer, "We are to glorify God."

I will ask them to tell me how to glorify God. The answers are all generic ones centered on religious activity. From direct praise and worship to attending church and reading our Bibles, I am giving a list that could be narrowed down to: Read your Bible, pray, go to church and try to get other people to....

It is amazing to me that God has told us in His word in direct terms with no room for misunderstanding how to glorify Him, yet I am never given that answer. Look back at John 15:8 again.

My Father is glorified by this, that you bear much fruit, and so prove to be My disciples. (John. 15.8)

If the goal of my life and the reason for my very existence is to glorify God and the way I glorify God is to bear much fruit, I should focus my life on bearing His fruit.

God chose us to be part of His spiritual orchard. He is the Husbandman, and we are His vineyard. People like to argue over election and predestination. I do not want to argue over how, but look clearly at the what. God chose us in order to bear His fruit. He did not elect us for heaven. He elected us for fruit. If we are not doing this, then we are not living in the written will of God.

Putting these things together, here is my working definition, followed by a phrase by phrase breakdown, of Spiritual Fruit.

Fruit is the Holy Spirit producing in me, and reproducing through me, the character and kingdom of God.

Fruit is the Holy Spirit...this is vital. We do not produce fruit. Fruit is not the result of a Bible study or small group event. It is not anything that we can do in our flesh. It is the by-product of our yielding to and being filled with the Holy Spirit. In the next chapter I will talk about the moment by moment walk, the abiding factor, of the Christian life. When we do this, abide in and be filled with the Holy Spirit, He produces the fruit in us. The illustration Jesus used in John 15 is classic. If you cut a branch off of a tree and throw it on the ground, it will not grow fruit. A branch does not grow fruit unless it is connected to the tree or the vine. The life of the vine flows into the branch, and fruit is the result.

Fruit is the Holy Spirit producing in me...God is at work in my life. I can see what He is doing as I see the fruit in my life. If you look back at all the spiritual fruits itemized in the Scripture, you discover that they reflect character growth and life change. God is at work in me.

Fruit is the Holy Spirit producing in me and reproducing

through me...God does not bless me so I will be blessed. He blesses me so I can be a blessing. One of the most important aspects of fruit is reproduction. God is not only at work in my life, He is at work through my life. God uses me. That results in my life affecting the lives of others. A great example of this is the teaching on His love. He gives me His love in order for me to love other people with it. I am blessed to be a blessing. I am not a reservoir where God's blessings are stored like the city water supply. I am a river of life where God's blessings flow to and through me to give life to others downstream.

Fruit is the Holy Spirit producing in me and reproducing through me the character...this is the obvious reading of the fruit. Moment by moment I am being transformed into the image of Christ. The Holy Spirit is conforming me to the image of Jesus Christ by producing the life of Christ in me through fruit. I am becoming like Him, not in my appearance, but in my character and bearing. I am adding moral excellence to my faith. As I disciple, mentor and train others to depend upon Christ and walk in the Holy Spirit, I am helping others in their own character growth. As I teach people to listen to the Holy Spirit and respond to Him, I am allowing God to not just produce in me, but reproduce through me, the character of Christ.

Fruit is the Holy Spirit producing in me, and reproducing through me, the character and kingdom of God....this last aspect deals with evangelism, missions and ministry in the church. God is at work, not just in my life and through my life, but by using me and my life in His church and His mission in the world. As I grow to be more like Christ, my passion will be what His is...world evangelism and discipleship. My goal is to bring all of my life under the reign and rule of the Father and to help others do the same.

TAIL WAGGING
THE DOG

After moving to Bolivia I discovered something about the way I taught and preached. I never knew it until then. I use a lot of pithy sayings and cultural proverbs. They just flow from my mouth. This is not an issue when I speak to people from my culture. The problem occurs if I am being translated into another language. I was teaching a conference for pastors before I learned Spanish. This necessitated a translator. During my message I used a saying I heard all my life growing up. I said, "Brothers, this is the tail wagging the dog." My translator stopped and looked at me. She said, "Pastor, I do not know what you mean." That was when I learned to focus on specific wording and not use colloquialisms or culture-based phrases. However, I do like the imagery of the tail wagging the dog. My mom said it a lot. This is how she said things were not in their proper order. She also stated that I had "Champagne taste on a beer pocketbook" and "The pot calling the kettle black", but those do not apply here. Neither does "You are staring like a calf at a new gate" and "That dog don't hunt". Oh, the joy of growing up a Texas redneck.

There are proverbs that show doing something incorrectly, applying the process wrongly, getting things out of order. I believe that in the Christian life; it is great to use the disciplines to help us know God better and love Him more. The problem is that we let the tail wag the dog, and we think practicing the disciplines *is* the goal. We do not grow by using spiritual discipline; we assume if we engage in the disciplines; we are growing. See the difference? There is an enormous contrast between doing the disciplines in order to grow and thinking the disciplines are growth.

I live in Cochabamba, Bolivia. In Bolivia there is a cool system of transportation called a Taxi Trufi. Imagine a bus route. The bus goes on this same route all day long, every day. If you want to go from where you are to another place; you need to take a bus that goes there. Instead of a bus, picture a compact economy car, designed to carry four people. This car has a number on top of it that tells you its route. You just flag the trufi down like a taxi. If less than eight people are inside this car designed for four, the trufi will pull over and you cram inside of it. You get in or out anywhere along the route that you desire. It is a hybrid of a bus and a taxi. It is super cheap. Taxi Trufi's are great.

Step into my life for a moment. I am on one side of the city, and I need to go to the bus terminal. What do I do? Knowing where I am and where I am going tells me which Taxi Trufi I need to stop. I choose the Trufi based on my destination. There may not be a trufi where you live, but you can understand the point using a bus or a subway, whichever you relate to best. You are in one location, and you want to go to another location. You can decide which line you need to take to arrive at your destination when you know your point of origin.

How often do you go to the bus stop and get on a bus, then ride it for the entire route and get off at the same stop? How many times have you taken a subway to the end of the line and then get on the return train? Do you ride the subway because other people ride it? No. Trufis, buses, and subways are all forms of transportation designed to carry you from point A to point B. They are not an end, they are a means to an end. Transit lines are a way to help you carry out your purpose of commuting.

The spiritual disciplines are a means to an end. They are not the purpose; they are to help us carry out a purpose. The methods are not the end. This is the heart of the problem. Somewhere along the way, we got the means confused with the end and the tail started trying to wag the dog. We started off using

Bible study to encounter God, and finished with, well, just Bible study. Although the Bible says that knowledge alone leads to pride while love edifies, all we do is study our Bible. We study our Bible because good Christians read their Bible. Bible reading has become the end, not the means to an end. It is as if we stopped riding the bus to get somewhere, and just started riding the bus. The purpose of our morning commute is to get on the bus. We ride it for forty-five minutes, then get off at the same stop. We have gone nowhere. Our lives have not changed. We have not moved forward. But we feel good because we rode the bus.

All of us have had this experience, and unfortunately many others have experienced this with us as the reference. Let me share my story. I once knew a man that was a super dee duper Christian. He was engaged in politics and culture. He was a pastor and a speaker. He was doctrinally sound and could not only teach all the doctrines and theologies of the Scripture, he could refute heresy. He could argue with a Mormon, Jehovah Witness, or a New Ager. He could prove his theological convictions with Scripture upon Scripture. He was honest, moral and faithful. He prayed with his family and avoided all the typical sins. He even ate organic foods! He read his Bible, prayed, went to church and tried to get other people.... He discipled and mentored men and other pastors. He was a leader in the denomination. He was well known, and to those who did not know him well, he was well liked.

Did you see that last sentence? He was well known, <u>and to those who did not know him well</u>, he was well liked. The more you got to know him, the less you liked him. From a distance, he was great. Up close was a different story. I once used this as an example to my children. I told them I believed we should live in such a way that those who know us best respect and love us the most. We should look better up close than far away. This man was the opposite. What was the problem?

He was mean, unforgiving, judgmental, arrogant, harsh, aggressive and divisive. He was opinionated about everything. He was unteachable. He never listened to opposing viewpoints. He was argumentative. He was a church leader and an example to others.

Isn't this a problem? Yet, you too have known someone like this, or it could be you are someone like this. I was. I was someone that knew their Bible, practiced the spiritual disciplines, and lived a moral lifestyle; yet was mean and unpleasant. How many of you have known mean Christians? It is amazing how we can self-identify as a follower of Jesus, yet we are nothing like Him. What is happening?

How can these Christian leaders be so diligent in their disciplines and so unlike Jesus in their attitudes? How can Christians talk so much about God's love and then be so hateful on social media? It is because they have stopped practicing the disciplines in order to love God more and allow the Holy Spirit to transform them into the image of Jesus. They practice the disciplines as part of a disciplined life. The disciplines have become the goal. They get on the prayer bus, and fifteen minutes later get off at the same stop. They have not progressed. They did not move. They did not gain any ground. They started at the corner of Stern and Grumpy and then got off at the same corner. They are no more like Jesus now than 15 years ago. They believe that praying and reading their Bible is what they and others should do and have forgotten that these are a tool to achieve something more. They think the tail wags the dog. The means has become the end.

Look at two verses with me.

And you shall love the Lord your God with all your heart, and with all your soul, and with all your mind, and with all your strength.' (Mark 12:30)

The commandment we are striving to do is to love God with all of our being. It is our purpose. This is our destination. There are things that we can do to get us there, forms of transportation so to speak, however the purpose is to love God. If what you are doing does not help you, encourage you, or enable you to love God more... why are you doing it? Do you love God more after your prayer than before you prayed?

But the goal of our instruction is love from a pure heart and a good conscience and a sincere faith. (1 Timothy 1:5)

I have a life purpose statement that I have written. This verse is the foundation of that purpose. The goal of our instruction is not to know more... it is to love more. I may take various forms of transportation, but I want to arrive at the corner of Love and Forgiveness. My destination determines my actions. Do we read the Bible, listen to messages and go to church to gain more knowledge of doctrine and church history, or to love God and others more? Are my disciplines helping me grow in love, or just in my ability to articulate what I believe and why others are wrong?

Therefore, we also have as our ambition, whether at home or absent, to be pleasing to Him. (2 Corinthians 5:9)

We have an ambition, a goal, and a purpose. That is to be pleasing to our Father. As in the above passages, we see steps that we can take to help us achieve our ambition, but the steps are *not the ambition*. Our ambition is not to read our Bibles and pray every day, it is to please God every day. Reading our Bibles can help us do that, but if they do not, what is it accomplishing?

But have nothing to do with worldly fables fit only for old women. On the other hand, discipline yourself for the purpose of godliness; (1 Timothy 4:7)

We are to discipline ourselves, but why? What is the purpose of our discipline? It is to be like Christ. The disciplines have a purpose, and that purpose is to change who we are. The disciplines are to transport us from here to there, not take us in a full circle where we arrive at the same place that we left.

Here is what I am saying. We have made a slight change that has wrecked our Christian lives. We have forgotten the purpose and now think the means to the end is the end. I am to pray, read my Bible, go to church fast, study, worship, etc., in order to do something else. Yet, we no longer focus on the something else, we do the something. We evaluate ourselves, not on whether we are reaching our destination, but on how comfortable is the bus ride. It doesn't matter if we are going anywhere. The important thing is that we got on the bus. We pray because good Christians pray. Obedient believers go to church. Mature Christians read their Bibles. We do _____ because we are supposed to do it. How do we evaluate our Christian life? We use quantitative measurements of how many bus rides we took. Good Christians take this bus every day. Period. I know you are a good Christian if I see you on my bus. Not only that, but being on my bus is the litmus test for life. We go nowhere. Our lives change little after the first two years of our Christian life, but we are on the bus.

I believe we can facilitate Christian growth through various actions. The point to emphasize is that doing them does not mean that I am growing in Christ. They are never to be the metric I choose to test my growth.

Pray in conduct to know God better and love Him more.

Go to church in order to know God better and love Him more.

Evangelize in order to help others know God better and love Him more.

Do not just follow the recipe and think you are cooking up Christlikeness. The disciplines are a means to an end. They are hypocrisy and legalism if doing them is your goal and not a means to your goal.

DISCIPLINES MAKE DISCIPLES

I am writing this chapter while flying to Ghana. I am on a mission trip with two of my sons, Caleb and Benjamin. We are going to Ghana to learn about micro-enterprise and finance from my friend Johnson. To get to Ghana, we have had to get a ride to our local airport and take a domestic flight to the city with the international airport. So, we flew from Cochabamba to Santa Cruz. At Santa Cruz, we had to take a taxi to a Missionary Guest House because the international flight did not leave until the next morning. The next morning, we took a taxi to the airport so we could arrive at the gate at 6:45 am. Our plane will take us to Miami, where we will change to British Airways and fly to Paris. In France we will switch to another plan and fly to Accra, Ghana. After spending the night in Accra at a missionary guest-house, we will go to the city of Tamale and stay at the Radach Memorial Center. Then, after a week, the reverse trip will take place.

So, why did I bore you with this worthless information? Well, the truth is, if I wanted to bore you, then I could have gone through all the steps and requirements that it takes to travel from a developing country if you are a resident alien, traveling with a minor, and on a passport not from the country you are coming from or going to. It took literally two weeks for us to get our documents and then three hours of paperwork at the airport just to leave the country! So, I spared you from this. Now, why tell you anything? Because we are just like you.

It is the destination that has determined so much of our lives for the last few months. Our destination determined which airlines, which flight, and what time. Our destination was the purpose behind our financial decisions, and which of my children traveled with me.

Remember the Taxi Trufi illustration? This applies to life. We were leaving Cochabamba, Bolivia to go to Tamale, Ghana. There are an infinite number of tasks and activities that we could have been doing for the past few months, but our destination influenced what we did. We eliminated options and made choices. The choices we made were to help us both arrive at our destination and enjoy the journey (hence the layover in Paris).

I believe there are things which can help us on our journey to become more like Christ, we must remember that these are steps in a journey to an ultimate destination. They are not why we do things. They are what we do in order to do a greater 'why'.

How do you describe the spiritual disciplines? I am not asking for a list, but for a definition. Here is my personal definition that I use and teach to others. I believe it is helpful to keep things in perspective.

Spiritual Disciplines are the Spirit-Led habits and activities that I do in order to know God better and love Him more.

Let's examine at this in detail. Every part of this definition is important for us to understand.

I was at the Texas State Fair one time, and my daughter wanted a puppy puppet. One of those items sold at places where people go expecting to throw money away. It was a "turkey leg" type of purchase. Seriously, where else do you spend your hard-earned money on baseball caps made of glow bracelets? My daughter saw the man making the little puppy jump around and dance and immediately wanted one. So, since we have a "once in your life I will buy you something stupid" policy for our kids, I bought her one. She made that little puppy walk around, jump, and dance. Until she put it in her closet and the strings got tangled up and then broke. I see her with that puppy and think this is what we try to do with the Holy Spirit. My prayer, Bible reading, or whatever is the little wooden handle that we attach the strings to. If I do it right, then I can make God dance to my tune. I can cause Him to leap up and answer my request, run around and bless my life. I pull the strings through my moral lifestyle, church attendance and discipline. This is the opposite of the Biblical teaching! God doesn't follow us. Discipleship is us following Him. A disciple is a follower. It is amazing that we try to follow God by leading Him. Habits are the SPIRIT LED things that I do. He leads me to read the Bible. He leads me to pray. I don't pray because I want to make God obey me. I pray in obedience to God.

Spirit-Led habits: This is the part of the disciplined life where we roam into legalism. I believe as we submit ourselves to the Holy Spirit, the clear teaching of the Bible is He works in our lives to change us into the image of Jesus. One way He does this is through the fruit of self-control. He will lead us to do things regularly. Jesus had habits. He went to the synagogue, "as was His custom" the Bible teaches. He prayed. He knew the Old Testament. The very first thing that Jesus did after beginning His ministry was to be "led of the Spirit" into the wilderness where He fasted (and by inference most likely prayed). God will probably lead you to do certain things regularly.

The danger is to believe that the things He leads you to do are the rule for all Christians, all the time, everywhere. For example, the Holy Spirit has led me to memorize, regularly, verses from the Bible. I also believe that God has led me to pray every day, and sometimes for prolonged periods. This does that mean that every believer in Jesus must spend an hour a day in prayer and memorize 10 verses a week. Another dangerous part of this aspect of Spiritual Discipline happens a lot. The Holy Spirit leads us to begin a certain habit. After a while, we think the habit is being led by the Spirit, so we stop seeking to hear Him. A spiritual habit should never become the substitute of a spiritual life.

Spirit-Led habits and activities: Some disciplines are habitual. They are a steady, daily, or in some form of regular occurrence. Others are more of an event. They do not take up a certain amount of time every morning, nor involve attending an event every week. They are activities that the Holy Spirit leads us to do. I believe that an excellent example of this is giving to the poor and fasting.

When we moved to Bolivia, the poorest country in all the Americas, we encountered true poverty. My family struggled with our response to the surrounding need. We could have given all of our money away the first week and not made a dent in the country. Yet, we know that the Biblical mandate includes helping the poor. After praying and fasting, and seeking advice from Godly people, we finally came up with this insightful plan. We would give to everyone that the Holy Spirit told us to give to. We give regularly to widows and young mothers living on the street. That is habitual. We give to orphans, kids living on the street and others as we sense the leadership of God. We give habitually to our local church. We give as an activity as God speaks to us.

Let me explain it with my wife as an example. We give more than a tithe as a spiritual habit. A short while ago, a missionary friend of mine and I were talking about a project of his. He is building a radio station that will broadcast Christian messages and songs to four distinct language groups. We helped him with the actual construction work. We discovered he was out of project money. He needed a little over $2,000 to build the first part of the living quarters. My wife felt the Holy Spirit tell her to meet this need. We are missionaries living on a budget. We come to your church and ask for money but, in response to the Holy Spirit, we gave $2500 to this project. We cannot give $2500 every week, month or year, but this time it was what God led us to do.

Fasting is another activity that God may lead us to. Without a doubt, we cannot fast every day or we will die. As a general practice, God has led us to fast regularly (habitual). God also leads us to fast for specific events at specific times for prolonged periods. We just finished a short fast as we were praying for a friend in ministry who recently left his wife and children. We fasted for his repentance. As we seek to hear God, there will be some things that, for us, should become habitual. Other things are eventful. The disciplined life comprises both. The focus is never to be on what we are doing but Who has called us to do it and how He wants us to do it.

Spirit-Led habits and activities that I do: This part does not need much explaining. Even though we are led by the Holy Spirit, we are not passive. We actively respond to Him. I must engage. The spiritual life is not one of quiet contemplation. It is a loud, noisy mess and busy life as I constantly do what God has led me to do. Sometimes we live as if there was a Greek dualism to life. We separate the spiritual from the secular, and the body from the spirit. Neither one of these are in the Bible. The body and the spirit are not the same thing, but they are intertwined in an inseparable Gordian knot. Even in eternity, at the final resurrection, God will join the body and the spirit once more. I challenge people in this area. Name one discipline I can do without my body and without my choice. Meditation requires my brain and thought, and both are physical. Prayer, giving, service, Bible reading, and church ministry all require physical activity. I cannot do something spiritual without my body, and it is good to remember that all the physical things I have my spirit and the Holy Spirit present. So, to be spiritually disciplined, I must physically respond to and participate with God.

Spirit-Led habits and activities that I do in order to know God better: There is a purpose in our disciplines, both the habitual and the periodic activity. It is to know God better. I am to grow in the grace and knowledge of our Lord. This is not Bible study. It is the purpose of Bible study. I don't study the Scripture so I will learn more doctrine. I study doctrine so I can comprehend more about God.

Spirit-Led habits and activities that I do in order to know God better and love Him more: I don't just do these things to stretch my brain, I do them to enlarge my heart. The goal of our instruction is love. Love the Lord your God with all. As we study and apply the Word, there is a purpose. It is to know and love God. I guess that this is probably one of the major themes of my teaching. We are to cooperate with the Holy Spirit as we grow in both knowledge and the love of God. If your activity, whether it is a daily, weekly or sporadic thing, does not increase your understanding of God and/or deepen your love for Him, then why are you doing it? That is the core. All that we do is to glorify Him. My purpose in life is to become like Jesus to the glory of God the Father. The Holy Spirit is in my life to make this happen. My purpose is not to be a fiscal conservative or a right wing political activist. It is not to be a moral person. It is not to be a religious fanatic. It is not to read my Bible, go to church, pray and try to get other people to read their bibles, etc. It is to cooperate with the Holy Spirit as He leads me to do things that help me become like Jesus Christ and glorify the Father.

I have written a discipleship program that I teach to Bolivian church leaders and pastors. It is the core of this book. I am writing what I say to pastors in one-on-one, small group and conference settings. I did a year long teaching series in my church based on what is in this book. Every week when I meet with the people I am discipling and I ask them this question:

Based upon what we have learned about God this week, is there anything in your life that God wants you to do. In response to Him, His Word or His Spirit, do you need to change something?

My goal is to cooperate with God as I try to help people learn to hear the voice and the guidance of the Holy Spirit. So, I try to avoid assignments. It isn't possible to not have any, because we all agree to study the same topic each week. However, I do all I can to let people hear from God instead of me. So, we study the chapter on the Scriptures. We learn what God says about it, how important it is to Jesus, that the Holy Spirit inspired it, that God has elevated it above His name. We see it is eternal, and it has all we need within it. We discover God has revealed His purpose and His heart inside of it. We wonder at the fact it is alive. Then we ask ourselves:

Based upon what we have learned about God this week, is there anything in your life God wants you to do. In response to Him, His Word or His Spirit, do you need to change something?

Is God satisfied with how I treat it?

Should I read it more than I do?

Does the Holy Spirit want me to memorize some particular passage, or maybe just memorize verses as a habit?

Is God telling me to change my daily routines, to incorporate this teaching and know Him better?

How can I love God more, and show my love, through what I now understand about His Word?

Guess what has happened to me 100% of the time in one-on-one meetings with about 70 different men? Every one of them told me God wanted them to read the Bible every day. They all started memorizing passages regularly. Each one of them said there were truths they wanted to meditate on. Many of the pastors felt the Holy Spirit wanted them to memorize the verses they were preaching on every week. Do you see the difference? I was discipled and taught to follow my teacher. In this way, we learn to listen to and follow God. In one, the standard becomes how I measure up to other people and/or complete my assignments. The other is whether I am responding to God's prompting for my life.

DO EVERYTHING

"Put it on a bumper sticker." That is what I was told by a mission committee I was meeting with to gain support for our ministry. The man that said it had asked me about our ministry and I was rambling on about all we were doing and how we were doing it. He wanted me to give him the core essence and nothing more. He rephrased it by saying, "What is your ministry Tweet?"

So, with discipleship, what is the tweet? What is on your discipleship bumper sticker? What is the one core thing that makes one a disciple?

If there were any one thing by which to define, defend and/or describe the successful Christian life I think it would be this one. I believe if we can teach ourselves to do this one thing, it will change our lives. If we would learn to ask ourselves this question, and answer it honestly, then we will not only be on the road to victory, but we will also live in victory. This question applies to every situation. It is useful in every relationship. It redeems every moment.

We find it all throughout the Bible. It is so important it is usually the first question-and-answer part of catechisms. For example, the famous Westminster Shorter Catechism begins with the question we need to ask ourselves as the answer.

The question is, "What is the chief end of man?". This is asking us to define success. Why is it we are even in existence? The answer given in the catechism is to glorify God and to enjoy Him forever. Here is how I phrase the question for my life and what I try to teach others to ask themselves.

"How can I bring God glory in this moment?"

"Are my thoughts glorifying God?"

"Will the words I want to say bring God honor?"

"What action can I do that will cause God to receive glory?"

Here is a driving verse. Look at it and think about what it is saying to us.

Whether, then, you eat or drink or whatever you do, do all to the glory of God. (1 Corinthians 10:31)

God gets the glory. Period. I am to think, speak, and act in such a manner that I glorify Him. Romans 3:23 sums up the sinful condition of man as 'fallen short of the glory of God'. God summarized sin by saying it was us not glorifying Him. If you contemplate the depth of this one verse, it will transform you. God says we should seek to glorify Him in every part of our lives, and even the mundane task of taking a drink of water can be and should be done for His glory. Over 500 times in the Bible, God uses the word 'glory' or one of its synonyms. We are to glorify God.

For you have been bought with a price: therefore glorify God in your body. (1 Corinthians 6:20)

If whatever you are doing involves your body, then it should be done for the glory of God. This means thinking, since it involves your brain and your mind, should glorify God. Your words, since they engage your physical body, should glorify God. Your actions, because it uses your body, should glorify God.

The successful disciple is someone who follows Jesus and does what He tells them to do in order to glorify God. A successful disciple is someone who seeks to glorify God in every aspect of their life at every moment of their life. When your desire and your efforts are to glorify God in your thoughts, words, attitudes, actions, relationships, roles and accomplishments, then you are being successful in every way.

Go back to the life-defining moment of the death of my

Son. His sudden death at 29 years of age rocked my world. My theology took a hit. My emotions were all over the board. My heart was and still is shattered by his loss.

As I was processing his death and preparing the message, I would give at his funeral, my mind was so full of questions. Let me share with you what I wrote in my journal and in my funeral message.

If we ask the wrong question, we will always end up at the wrong answer. We have to focus on the correct question. When an unexpected and tragic death hits you, the first question you ask again and again is this: Why did this happen? That question is a terrible question. The reason it is not a good question is because there is no answer that will help you. I heard so many platitudes in the weeks and months of his death. Most of them made me want to throw up because they were meaningless chatter. One phrase thrown out over and over is, "God has a purpose in this." It is also phrased in a guess what God's purpose is such as "I just know someone will come to Christ because of Seth's death."

The problem is that I know God has an infinite number of resources at His disposal. He did not have to kill my son to accomplish some little detail in His grand scheme of the universe. If He wanted one of my son's friends to come to Christ, then He could have used a friend sharing the gospel, a tract, a radio program, a childhood memory, a Bible verse, or a friend at work. You name it. He did not have to kill Seth to bring life to someone. When a parent loses a child, I promise you no reason will make them say, "Okay God, I understand. It is cool. Do You want to take another of my kids since it makes so much sense?"

Asking why serves no purpose except to leave you with emptiness and/or an anger or resentment at God. Asking why causes you to fill up the emptiness of no sufficient answer with bitterness. The devil gets you to ask why to cause you to question the love and/or power of God. Since there is no reason for this to have HAD to have happened, why did God let it? God must not love me. These attacks on God come from the poor question, "Why".

Another set of questions are in the 'What Now' category. These are task-oriented things that have to be done in order to have the funeral and all the details around a death. These questions do not help you deal with the crisis. They help you manage tasks the crisis created. These are not good or bad, they just are necessary.

The best question to ask in a time like this is: "How can I respond to this horrible tragedy in a way that will bring glory to God?" We need to move beyond what has happened and seek avenues on how to glorify God after it has happened. I do not want to be an embittered parent who has lost a child. I want to be a grieving father pointing others to the glory of God.

That is the reason I wrote the book "How Could My Son Be Dead?". I hoped people could see how we continue(d) to plod through the worst day/month/year of our life with a sincere desire to Glorify our Father.

I was/am grieving. I want my grief to bring Him glory.

I am broken by his death. I want my broken and shattered heart to reflect Him. I want my children to see God is worthy, and God is good even when life truly stinks. My life is not about my plans succeeding. My life is to be about the glory of God. My son dies, and God is still worthy of Glory. My heart breaks, and God is still worthy of Glory. His death is horrible. God is still worthy of Glory.

Life is not about getting the 'How To' checklists all finished so you can be super productive. It is not about understanding the deep and profound reasoning behind various philosophical discussions. Life is about the glory of God.

In our marriage workshops, we often teach on conflict and how to manage it. The first principle we explain is we are to glorify God. This conflict and how I respond to it is to glorify God. When my wife disagrees with me, the thoughts that go through my mind should be taken captive and brought into the obedience of Christ so the very thoughts I have about her, the event, the conflict and my answer should glorify Him. My words, both what I say and how I say them, in the very heated moment of the conflict itself, should be a balm to Christ and honor Him. My actions toward the conflict, the cause of the conflict and my wife and/or anyone else in the conflict should minister grace and love to the glory of God.

What would happen to your marriage if you asked these simple questions both proactively and in response to others?

"How can I bring God glory in this moment?"

"Are my thoughts glorifying God?"

"Will the words I want to say bring God honor?"

"What action can I do that will cause God to receive glory?"

What would happen in your parenting, and in the relationships you have with your children, if you examined your role as a parent considering these questions? Imagine you are encouraging your child, or you are disciplining them for their behavior and as you did it, these questions went through your mind:

"How can I bring God glory in this moment?"

"Are my thoughts glorifying God?"

"Will the words I want to say bring God honor?"

"What action can I do that will cause God to receive glory?"

List every role and relationship you have. You are a parent, child, sibling, cousin, friend, church member, employee, employer, co-worker, neighbor, citizen, etc. Now, in every one of those roles and relationships, what would happen if you asked those questions?

Go back to that verse.

"Whether, then, you eat or drink or whatever you do, do all to the glory of God." (1 Corinthians 10:31)

The first part of being a true follower of Christ is to realize as you are following Him, you are also pointing to Him. When people look at you and your life, they should see Christ being magnified.

The very first and the core component of real discipleship is learning in this moment every fiber of my being exists to glorify my Father Who is in heaven. Remember the focus of being a disciple and of being a disciple maker is the Presence and Person of Jesus Christ. He is here and worthy of being glorified right now, and it is always right now.

THE WORD

About 20 years ago, I told my wife I wanted to learn how to play the piano. I have always enjoyed music. I have a very eclectic taste. I like and respect all the genres and appreciate the art itself. So, I wanted to learn to play the piano. She agreed to teach me. We started with a few basic chords and reading music. She taught me the different lines on a sheet of music and what the various notes signified. I learned about bass and treble clefs. She is a great teacher. However, after less than three weeks of her teaching me, I quit. I told her, "I misspoke. I do not want to learn how to play the piano. I want to play the piano. The learning part is what I do not want to do. So, I will stop the lessons now. My desire to play the piano is not worth the work of learning to play the piano." I never took another lesson.

I was being honest. Many times in our lives we have desires. There are things we want. We would like to do some skill or to know some knowledge. We want to have an experience or an accomplishment. We do not develop the skill or take the class. We do not go on the trip or accomplish our desire. The reason we do not do it is simple. The goal was not worth the effort it took to attain. It is a nice thing to hold out as desirable, but not worthy enough to do what it takes to fulfill that desire. Like me, you want to play piano but not learn to play piano. We want the destination but do not want to take the journey. The sad truth is life does not work like that. I cannot go to where I want to be without leaving where I am and doing what it takes to get me there.

In every area of life, those that are successful became that way by doing what it took to get successful. I read a meme that said, "Motivation is worthless. Discipline is priceless." There is not a single professional athlete that became the level of player they are on raw talent alone. They had to practice and drill repeatedly for decades. The highest-level musicians did not master their instrument by ear. They practice the simple chords until they are natural and then add more and more complex drills until it is muscle memory. They practice. Whether it is in the world of arts, business or sports, the people at the top got there by one thing in common. They have and used discipline.

This is true in your spiritual growth as well. We must be disciplined. There are things we should do over and over until we ingrain them into our lives like muscle memory. The important thing is we keep the end in mind. Musicians don't practice simple chords in order to play the chords. They do it to accomplish much greater things.

We are disciples. That implies we are disciplined. Discipline leads us to practice some basic disciplines of growth. When we are disciplined, we are allowing God to lead you into a lifestyle that promotes growth. Stay focused on our working definition of the spiritual disciplines.

Spiritual Disciplines are the Spirit-Led habits and activities that I do in order to know God better and love Him more.

I believe one area God will lead us is in the habit of consuming Bible reading and study. I intentionally did not use the words "daily Bible reading and study" on purpose. I believe one can see in Scripture and in the lives of the saints in the Bible and history, that a true disciple becomes consumed with consuming God's word. We should be immersed in His word. As in most of these things, we have substituted the best for something that is not bad. Instead of being consumed with the word and reading large portions with in-depth study, we have devotional booklets. We read one verse and then a page of the author's thoughts about the verse. We have our fifteen-minute quiet times. I cannot stand devotionals. They reduce God's word down to a platitude and minimize our engagement with it. A follower of Christ ought to follow the Words of Christ, not what someone else says about them. If we are really spiritual, we will read the Proverb of the day. I am not talking about skipping across the surface of the Bible. I mean we should scuba dive into it. We should immerse ourselves. We should seek to know it inside and out. I want to brag on my wife. In 2006, we were planning on going to the mission field. Denise has never taken a single Bible course in any official capacity. I say that to set up this true story. The mission agency we went with required us to take a 400 question Bible exam. The purpose was to evaluate our Biblical knowledge and to determine if any additional study was needed. Denise scored a 96% on her test. She is a full-time wife and mother with no formal Bible training. She knows her Bible. This is because she immerses herself in God's Word. In 2018 and 2019, she attempted to read the Bible in its entirety once a month. She told me she failed and only read it 10 times in 2019. That is 10 times from Genesis to Revelation in one year. She does this because it is GOD's Word! Here are some reasons I believe God will lead other disciples to become disciplined in the Word as He has me.

First, notice how important God's Word is to Him.

I will bow down toward Your holy temple and give thanks to Your name for Your lovingkindness and Your truth; for You have magnified Your word according to all Your name. (Psalm 138:2)

The word translated 'according' can also mean 'above, or with'. God is saying that as awesome and incredible is His Name is, His word is right beside it. He elevates His word to the status of His name or His character itself.

In the beginning was the Word, and the Word was with God, and the Word was God. (John 1:1)

When our children were born, we spent a lot of time thinking about what name to give to them. We first chose a Biblical theme. We then looked at the meanings of various names and what we wanted their name to communicate. God gave us boys first, so we named them in order: Seth, Jacob, Caleb, Benjamin, David and Joshua. We taught them the foundation of their names. Our girls followed, and they were named Faith, Hope, Joy, Patience and Mercy. We have emphasized what their names mean to them as well, and why we chose their particular name. Look at this verse. No one gave God a name. He named Himself. He could have named Himself anything in or out of creation. When He named Himself, the name He chose before giving Himself the name "The One Who Saves", was "The Word". His name for Himself is the "Word". This reveals to us how important the Word is. It is what He calls Himself!

Heaven and earth will pass away, but My words will not pass away. (Matthew 24:35)

God's word is important to us because of what it is.

But know this first of all, that no prophecy of Scripture is a matter of one's own interpretation, for no prophecy was ever made by an act of human will, but men moved by the Holy Spirit spoke from God. (2 Peter 1:20-21)

You, however, continue in the things you have learned and become convinced of, knowing from whom you have learned them, and that from childhood you have known the sacred writings which are able to give you the wisdom that leads to salvation through faith which is in Christ Jesus. All Scripture is inspired by God and profitable for teaching, for reproof, for correction, for training in righteousness; so that the man of God may be adequate, equipped for every good work. (2 Timothy 3:14-17)

God's word is inspired. That means we have in our hands a book that was literally written by God! In 2000, Denise and

I began a practice we will continue until the day we die. We wrote a letter to our children for them to read after we die. It is called "Hey, I Died". I have expanded it and I have also written a letter to Denise for her to read if I die before her. When writing these letters, we imagined our children holding them in their hands a week or so after the funeral. They are about to open them and read them for the first, but most likely not the only, time. How do you think they will feel? How important to both them and to us do you think the words, the content and the stories in those letters are? God wrote a letter to us. He literally put His heart and His mind on paper and give it to us to read. If it was so important to God to write, don't you think it should be important to us to read and understand?

God's word is important to us because of what it does.

But He answered and said, "It is written, 'Man shall not live on bread alone, but on every word that proceeds out of the mouth of God.'" (Matthew 4:4)

For the word of God is living and active and sharper than any two-edged sword, and piercing as far as the division of soul and spirit, of both joints and marrow, and able to judge the thoughts and intentions of the heart (Hebrews 4:12)

For as the rain and the snow come down from heaven, and do not return there without watering the earth and making it bear and sprout, and furnishing seed to the sower and bread to the eater; So will My word be which goes forth from My mouth; It will not return to Me empty, without accomplishing what I desire, and without succeeding in the matter for which I sent it. (Isaiah 55:10-11)

How can a young man keep his way pure? By keeping it according to Your word. With all my heart I have sought You; Do not let me wander from Your commandments. Your word I have treasured in my heart, that I may not sin against You. (Psalm 119:9-11)

For whatever was written in earlier times was written for our instruction, so that through perseverance and the encouragement of the Scriptures we might have hope. (Romans 15:4)

Sanctify them in the truth; Your word is truth. (John 17:17)

So faith comes from hearing, and hearing by the word of Christ. (Romans 10:17)

for you have been born again not of seed which is perishable but imperishable, that is, through the living and enduring word of God. (1 Peter 1:23)

You, however, continue in the things you have learned and become convinced of, knowing from whom you have learned them, and that from childhood you have known the sacred writings which are able to give you the wisdom that leads to salvation through faith which is in Christ Jesus. All Scripture is inspired by God and profitable for teaching, for reproof, for correction, for training in righteousness; so that the man of God may be adequate, equipped for every good work. (2 Timothy 3:14-17)

Read and reread those passages. It is God's word that transforms us into His image and will. His word reveals who we are. His word teaches us what we should do. His word expresses His desire for our heart and soul. His word gives us wisdom and truth. His word gives us salvation. His word accomplishes His will. His word is His desire for us.

As you see how important God's word is to Him and how important it is to us, how can one not become consumed with knowing it in as minute detail as possible? Therefore, I believe a disciple will become consumed with His word.

We want to glorify God in every thought. His word teaches us how to think and renews our mind.

We want to glorify God in our actions. His word reveals to us how we should live our lives in this fallen world and what our priorities should be.

We want to glorify God in our relationships. His word teaches us how to live with and love other people.

We want to glorify God in our words. His word teaches us where our words originate and how to express ourselves.

God's word is how He has and will reveal His heart to us and His will for us. It is only through knowing His word that we can truly know Him. A disciple is someone who follows Jesus and does what He tells them to do. His word and His Spirit using His word is how He tells us what to do. The focus of discipleship is the Presence and Person of Jesus Christ. His word teaches us Who the Person of Jesus Christ is and what He is like.

I believe as we seek to become wholehearted disciples of Jesus Christ, we will be led by the Holy Spirit to become habitual in our study and application of God's word.

GIVING

We have homeschooled our children for over 25 years. In the process there are things we have learned are important. For example, we insist our kids learn their addition and multiplication facts perfectly and that they can recite them instantly without thought. They have to answer the math fact question before I finish asking it. This is because we have learned these are the key to doing more advance mathematics. We have our kids learn broad historical periods and key characters, but we do not have them memorize very many dates. We focus on our children reading well, but we do not take a lot of time diagraming sentences because we have not seen the benefit of it. I am confident that when I told you what we did not do, some readers immediately disagreed with our opinion on it. Some think memorizing pivotal dates in history is important to an excellent education. Others think diagramming is the key to good grammar. Everyone has their opinion on which part of the educational system should be focused upon. The same is true with the disciplines. Everyone has an opinion or a thought on which disciplines should be included in any discipleship course. For example, almost all authors include the discipline of Bible reading, while virtually no one focuses on the discipline of solitude. As I designed my course, I knew I would not write another one of those "Read your Bible, pray, go to church and try to get other people to read, etc." programs. Yet, there are disciplines that are the blocking and tackling of our faith.

I decided to just include four. I included the first one on Bible consumption, and the reasons for it are in the previous chapter. The next three I chose because Jesus used them as His examples in the Sermon on the Mount. He told His disciples how to do these three disciplines. If they were important enough for Him to teach, then I believe we should consider them important enough for us to teach and to do. As you read this, keep in mind our definition of the disciplines.

Spiritual Disciplines are the Spirit-Led habits and activities that I do in order to know God better and love Him more.

I believe that since Jesus taught these things and then the Holy Spirit inspired Matthew to record them, we can assume that the Holy Spirit will lead us to do them.

Beware of practicing your righteousness before men to be noticed by them; otherwise you have no reward with your Father who is in heaven. So when you give to the poor, do not sound a trumpet before you, as the hypocrites do in the synagogues and in the streets, so that they may be honored by men. Truly I say to you, they have their reward in full. But when you give to the poor, do not let your left hand know what your right hand is doing, so that your giving will be in secret; and your Father who sees what is done in secret will reward you. (Matthew 6:1-4)

The first of the disciplines mentioned is that of giving and I want to add the adverb generously to that based upon more teaching from the Bible outside of this passage. So, the first discipline that we should pursue is the discipline of generosity.

So when you give to the poor, do not sound a trumpet before you, as the hypocrites do in the synagogues and in the streets, so that they may be honored by men. Truly I say to you, they have their reward in full. But when you give to the poor, do not let your left hand know what your right hand is doing, so that your giving will be in secret; and your Father who sees what is done in secret will reward you. (Matthew 6:2-4)

I believe that we pastors have done a huge disservice to the church. I ascribe it to pure motivation. We want our churches to have money to operate. We want to fund our programs. We want to pay our bills. We want to feed our families. These things need money. Therefore, we have gone to our churches and emphasized how important it is to tithe. We teach tithing as either a law from Moses that remains in effect under grace or as an overarching principle throughout the Bible. My pastor taught me the tithe was a spiritual principle that did not begin or end with Moses. He taught me I must tithe, or I was in sin. Pastors stress tithing. They threaten people with dire consequences if they do not tithe. If you do not tithe God will in some form punish you by making your car need repairs or your home maintenance bill increase. If you tithe, then your car won't break down. We pound tithing over and over into our church members' ears. However, when Jesus talked to His disciples about giving, He did not use the tithe as His example. He used giving to the poor as an example. That is being generous.

I have two issues with the emphasis on tithing. The first one we can disagree on if you feel the Bible teaches differently. I believe that tithing is not mandatory. I do not believe that we are under any aspect of the civil law of Moses. I do not think animal sacrifices ended, but the tithe held on. I think tithing is no longer a command for God's people. The second reason I disagree with this forced tithe teaching is I think it undermines God's intention for us. It does not teach us to be generous. Our mentors instruct us on how to be rule followers. We do not learn to listen to the Holy Spirit regarding our finances. Instead, we learn how to multiply by 10%. We are just expected to tithe. If there is an offering for some other thing in a church, we don't call for generosity. We call for people to make sure they tithe before they give. It is "above and beyond your normal tithe" is how we say it.

As a missionary, I experience this teaching a lot when I visit churches. Many times, the pastor will tell me that while I can share my ministry, I can in no way ask for financial support. At times I am prohibited from passing out prayer cards since they include information on how to give. These pastors think that their congregation is not generous and therefore they must guard the vault. Other times after presenting the pastor will stress, "If God leads you to give to the Holmans, after your normal tithe to the church, then please do so." Once more, the assumption is that the church member will not be generous, and it might tempt them to rob Peter to pay Paul. The pastor emphasizes tithing and mentions giving.

I believe that if God, under the law, mandated a 10% church tax, then we under grace would want to give more. In my personal discipleship as I teach about Biblical finances, I challenge people to ask the Holy Spirit if 10% is nearly enough to classify them as generous givers.

Giving is so important that God addresses it in detail in 2 Corinthians. God dedicated two chapters of this book to the spiritual discipline of giving generously. Here is the context as you read the passage. Through persecution and famine, the church in Jerusalem had become poor and in need. Paul had told the Corinthian church about their brothers and sisters elsewhere, and the church decided to give money to them. They surprised Paul by how generous they would give. In His own words they were giving *'beyond their ability'*. They were not just giving out of what they could, they were giving beyond what they could. He tried to talk them out of giving so much. Their insistence on being so generous was the context that the Holy Spirit used to teach us about generosity.

Now, brethren, we wish to make known to you the grace of God which has been given in the churches of Macedonia, that in a great ordeal of affliction their abundance of joy and their deep poverty overflowed in the wealth of their liberality. For I testify that according to their ability, and beyond their ability, they gave of their own accord, begging us with much urging for the favor of participation in the support of the saints, and this, not as we had expected, but they first gave themselves to the Lord and to us by the will of God. So we urged Titus that as he had previously made a beginning, so he would also complete in you this gracious work as well. But just as you abound in everything, in faith and utterance and knowledge and in all earnestness and in the love we inspired in you, see that you abound in this gracious work also. I am not speaking this as a command, but as proving through the earnestness of others the sincerity of your love also. For you know the grace of our Lord Jesus Christ, that though He was rich, yet for your sake He became poor, so that you through His poverty might become rich. I give my opinion in this matter, for this is to your advantage, who were the first to begin a year ago not only to do this, but also to desire to do it. But now finish doing it also, so that just as there was the readiness to desire it, so there may be also the completion of it by your ability. For if the readiness is present, it is acceptable according to what a person has, not according to what he does not have. For this is not for the ease of others and for your affliction, but by way of equality— at this present time your abundance being a supply for their need, so that their abundance also may become a supply for your need, that there may be equality; as it is written, "He who gathered much did not have too much, and he who gathered little had no lack." But thanks be to God who puts the same earnestness on your behalf in the heart of Titus. For he not only accepted our appeal, but being himself very earnest, he has gone to you of his own accord. We have sent along with him the brother whose fame in the things of the gospel has spread through all the churches; and not only this, but he has also been appointed by the churches to travel with us in this gracious work, which is being administered by us for the glory of the Lord Himself, and to show our readiness, taking precaution so that no one will discredit us in our administration of this generous gift; for we have regard for what is honorable, not only in the sight of the Lord, but also in the sight of men. We have sent with them our brother, whom we have often tested and found diligent in many things, but now even more diligent because of his great confidence in you. As for Titus, he is my partner and fellow worker among you; as for our brethren, they are messengers of the churches, a glory to Christ. Therefore openly before the churches, show them the proof of your love and of our reason for boasting about you. For it is superfluous for me to write to you about this ministry to the saints; for I know your readiness, of which I boast about you to the Macedonians, namely, that Achaia has been prepared since last year, and your zeal has stirred up most of them. But I have sent the brethren, in order that our boasting about you may not be made empty in this case, so that, as I was saying, you may be prepared; otherwise if any Macedonians come with me and find you unprepared, we—not to speak of you—will be put to shame by this confidence. So I thought it necessary to urge the brethren that they would go on ahead to you and arrange beforehand your previously promised bountiful gift, so that the same would be ready as a bountiful gift and not affected by covetousness. Now this I say, he who sows sparingly will also reap sparingly, and he who sows bountifully will also reap bountifully. Each one must do just as he has purposed in his heart, not grudgingly or under compulsion, for God loves a cheerful giver. And God is able to make all grace abound to you, so that always having all sufficiency in everything, you may have an abundance for every good deed; as it is written, "He scattered abroad, he gave to the poor, his righteousness endures forever." Now He who supplies seed to the sower and bread for food will supply and multiply your seed for sowing and increase the harvest of your righteousness; you will be enriched in everything for all liberality, which through us is producing thanksgiving to God. For the ministry of this service is not only fully supplying the needs of the saints, but is also overflowing through many thanksgivings to God. Because of the proof given by this ministry, they will glorify God for your obedience to your confession of the gospel of Christ and for the liberality of your contribution to them and to all, while they also, by prayer on your behalf, yearn for you because of the surpassing grace of God in you. Thanks be to God for His indescribable gift! (2 Corinthians 8:1-9:15)

Another thing to see is that giving flows from the Presence and Person of God. The focus of being a disciple and of being a disciple maker is the Presence and Person of Jesus Christ. A disciple as someone who follows Jesus and does what He tells them to do. Giving reflects the character of Christ. They could give so much of their money to the work of God because they had already given so much of their lives to God. God said that they first gave themselves to the Lord. It was because of this act of surrender and worship of themselves that they could then give and to us by the Will of God. The Holy Spirit inspired Paul to refer to the very life of Christ as our example in giving.

For you know the grace of our Lord Jesus Christ, that though He was rich, yet for your sake He became poor, so that you through His poverty might become rich.

Instead, as we live in the Presence of Christ with Him as our example, He will work in us and then we can do just as he has purposed in his heart, not grudgingly or under compulsion, for God loves a cheerful giver. God working in our lives allows our giving to no longer just be a rule. Pastors do not need to manipulate us into donating. Instead, we share from a heart of laughter. Our grateful hearts give generously to the glory of God. All of this comes from focusing on the Person and Presence of Jesus Christ.

Now He who supplies seed to the sower and bread for food will supply and multiply your seed for sowing and increase the harvest of your righteousness; you will be enriched in everything for all liberality, which through us is producing thanksgiving to God. For the ministry of this service is not only fully supplying the needs of the saints, but is also overflowing through many thanksgivings to God. Because of the proof given by this ministry, they will glorify God for your obedience to your confession of the gospel of Christ and for the liberality of your contribution to them and to all, while they also, by prayer on your behalf, yearn for you because of the surpassing grace of God in you. Thanks be to God for His indescribable gift!

I start off by asking, "Do you truly believe the Bible?". They always affirm it, so then I turn to this passage. In everything I showed you that by working hard in this manner you must help the weak and remember the words of the Lord Jesus, that He Himself said,

It is more blessed to give than to receive. (Acts 20:35).

I then say. "The Bible plainly teaches that it is more blessed to give than to receive. If I can motivate you to give to my ministry, then I have led you into a deeper blessing by your giving than I will have by my receiving. That is the Bible. Think about it. If you give to our ministry: You get to take part in the Kingdom work of God. You are growing in the virtue of generosity. You are mimicking the character of Jesus Christ. You are following the leading of the Holy Spirit. You are investing in the eternal destinies of the souls of men. God has promised your investment to grow by 1,000 percent for all eternity. You are laying up treasures in heaven. You are refocusing your heart and overcoming the sins of coveting and idolatrous greed. I can buy food for my kids. It is more blessed to give than to receive. So, let me help you be more blessed and me be blessed. How much money do you want to donate to our ministry and the work of God?"

This is not manipulation. It is Bible. The church in 2 Corinthians understood it. That is why they begged to give. Giving generously is a privilege open to all socio-economic levels. God measures it by the widow's mite, not the rich man's wealth. Even though they were begging to give, God spend the first five verses of chapter nine reminding and encouraging them to give. I am courageous as I challenge my church and my donors to give to the work of God because I know beyond any doubt that in teaching them to give, I am blessing them. Denise and I are missionaries living on the support of God's people. We are also givers. We support five other missionaries in four other countries and give a large percentage of our income to the church and to help the poor. I once shared with one of our donating churches how much we gave and the initial response was incredulity. This was followed by the idea that if we could give as much away as we did we must not need as much support as we were receiving. I took a few minutes to show them you do not give out of abundance or overflow. You give out of an abundance of joy and of sacrifice. We do not give a large percentage away because we have so much left over afterwards. We give to God's work because it is good to do so. That leads to the next reason to be generous.

Giving is a virtue that God has told us to develop and mature. Look at what God said.

But just as you abound in everything, in faith and utterance and knowledge and in all earnestness and in the love we inspired in you, see that you abound in this gracious work also.

In the same way that we grow in our faith, teaching, knowledge, sincerity and love we should see that you abound in this gracious work also. God wants us to abound in our giving. It is as important as abounding in other virtues. He even connects giving generously with the virtue of love. Our giving reveals our love.

At the end of Chapter 8 he said:

Therefore openly before the churches, show them the proof of your love.

Our generosity shows the sincerity of and proves our love. The most practical illustration of this is what God did.

For God so loved the world, that He gave His only begotten Son, that whoever believes in Him shall not perish, but have eternal life. (John 3:16)

God loves us and GAVE His Son.

It is no mistake that when Jesus taught His disciples about spiritual disciplines that the first one He taught was that of giving generously.

PRAYER

In 1994, my wife and I had the only bump in the road in our relationship. After discovering things were not as they should be and seeking to find out why we were not as close as we once were, we discovered the core issue was a lack of communication. Our conversations had become news reports of our day. I told her things related to my job, and she told me things about the kids, and we balanced chores at home. There was no actual communication as there had been in the past. We worked on it together. We made a decision that when I came home from the office each day, we would teach the kids to not interrupt us and we would talk for at least 15 minutes. We had a rule. She could not talk about the children, and I could not talk about the church. It was embarrassing. The first day we looked at each other for a few minutes and I said, "I am sorry to say, I got nothing. I truly have nothing to say to you. I don't know what to talk about." She did not either. After 10 years of marriage, we had nothing to say. Our relationship was one with no conflict. We were not fighting. We coexisted as managers of the Holman household. We ended up purchasing conversation starter books to help us. Fast-forward to the present day. This is not a hyperbole. I am not exaggerating. We talk together at least two hours a day. We talk about everything all the time. We are in constant and open communication. We communicate more than anyone I know, and I believe because of that we have a better relationship than anyone I know. In our marriage conferences we share this story with many more details, and we teach on how to communicate. Over the years as we talked, something happened. We learned to talk. We discovered an openness. We grew in our ability to understand each other. We talked more and more until there is no time limit on how much or how little we talk. We talk. I bring this up because I believe this is the key and often neglected component of the next discipline Jesus taught His disciples.

Spiritual Disciplines are the Spirit-Led habits and activities that I do in order to know God better and love Him more.

Beware of practicing your righteousness before men to be noticed by them; otherwise you have no reward with your Father who is in heaven. So when you give to the poor, do not sound a trumpet before you, as the hypocrites do in the synagogues and in the streets, so that they may be honored by men. Truly I say to you, they have their reward in full. But when you give to the poor, do not let your left hand know what your right hand is doing, so that your giving will be in secret; and your Father who sees what is done in secret will reward you. When you pray, you are not to be like the hypocrites; for they love to stand and pray in the synagogues and on the street corners so that they may be seen by men. Truly I say to you, they have their reward in full. But you, when you pray, go into your inner room, close your door and pray to your Father who is in secret, and your Father who sees what is done in secret will reward you. And when you are praying, do not use meaningless repetition as the Gentiles do, for they suppose that they will be heard for their many words. So do not be like them; for your Father knows what you need before you ask Him. Pray, then, in this way: Our Father who is in heaven, Hallowed be Your name. Your kingdom come. Your will be done, on earth as it is in heaven. Give us this day our daily bread. And forgive us our debts, as we also have forgiven our debtors. And do not lead us into temptation but deliver us from evil. For Yours is the kingdom and the power and the glory forever. Amen.' For if you forgive others for their transgressions, your heavenly Father will also forgive you. But if you do not forgive others, then your Father will not forgive your transgressions. (Matthew 6:5-15)

Jesus talked more about prayer than the other two disciplines combined. Prayer is a vital component of following Christ. A disciple is someone who follows Jesus and does what He tells them to do. He told us to pray. The focus of being a disciple and of being a disciple maker is the Presence and Person of Jesus Christ. This is really the heart of prayer. I understand I am in the Presence of Jesus Christ, and so I talk to Him. I want to talk to Him, and He says, "I am right here." As with so many other things in the Bible, we have taken an incredibly simple truth and made it into a huge theological mumbo jumbo. We have Bible studies on the components of prayer. We discuss the difference between intercession and petition. We give brief outlines on prayer to make sure we cover all of our bases.

What if, and this may seem strange to you, but what if prayer was little different from talking to each other? What if prayer was mainly us talking to God about His plans and our lives? What if prayer was us recognizing the Person of God and therefore worshipping Him for Who He Is and talking to Him because He is Present with us at the moment? What if the real backbone of prayer was constantly realizing Jesus is with me and therefore talking and listening to Him about everything going on in my life? Can you see if we do not complicate prayer, it is really a simple task? Prayer is communicating with the God Who is right here.

I first realized prayer was easy in Seminary. It was not in a class. It was in my commute. I lived in a suburb of Fort Worth, Texas. I went to seminary in Fort Worth. I worked in Arlington. My commute was almost like a triangle. I drove to seminary, from seminary to the night shift at General Motors and back to my home in Mansfield. I spent around one and a half hours a day on the road. We were seeking to save up as much money as we could and living on a tight budget. We went through college and seminary debt free. The reason I am telling you this is my car was a 25-year-old junker. It only had three gears. It had neutral, second gear and park. I could not drive over 45, even on the interstate. I always parked in a spot that let me pull in and drive forward out of it since I did not have reverse. It did not have air conditioning or heat, nor did it have a radio. It had two positive features. It was owned free and clear. It went from point A to point B. One day I was driving, and I saw a horrific accident on the other side of the road. I instantly prayed for the people and all involved. I continued to pray for the rest of my commute, which was about 15 minutes. The Holy Spirit spoke to me in this time. I realized instead of driving in silence and daydreaming due to the lack of radio, I could talk to my Father.

I started praying every single time I was in the car alone. I talked to Him. I asked Him to work in the lives of people I worked with and in my network. I talked to Him about His plans for my life and asked Him questions. I talked to Him about verses I memorized and asked Him to help me understand them. I talked to Him about current events. I told Him about my life and my struggles. I asked for advice. I listened to Him as I asked for Scripture to guide me.

Go back and look at that paragraph again because after using the word "praying" in the first sentence, I intentionally never used it again. I talked, asked and listened. I would imagine He was in the passenger seat, although in reality He was much closer. I talked out loud. I asked Him to reveal Himself to people who passed me or whom I passed. I asked Him to protect people driving dangerously. I sought for Him to give wisdom to parents as I saw them driving with children or evidence of children in the car. I asked Him to bring salvation to pedestrians as I drove past. I talked. I listened and talked. It was simple communication. I did not divide my prayer into segments like confession, petition, intercession, supplication and whatnot. I don't do that with my wife. I don't do that with my friends. My conversation roams from one subject to another and from shallow to deep. So do my prayers.

I continued this simple prayer life until the present day. I often walk for exercise. If my wife doesn't go with me, I will chat with God the entire time. People who see me in the present think I have a blue tooth conversation going on my phone. In the past, they assumed I was crazy and talking to myself.

I also have times of closet prayer. This is the prayer most people refer to when they discuss praying. However, in my devotion I have demystified prayer. I typically start off listening to what my Father is saying through His word. I have a journal and I write a small greeting to God and ask Him to speak to me through His word. I read the passage of Scripture, praying as I read it and jotting down any insights. I turn on worship music and sing and sometimes dance before Him. I almost always end up with my face on the floor in worship as the result of God revealing His Majesty to me. I talk about everything. I thank Him for anything that comes to my mind. I pray for my family. I ask God to save people. I do all the 'official prayer' stuff. I do it in a flowing conversational manner that also involves sitting and listening to His Holy Spirit and Word. For example, I may ask Him if there is anyone whom I should contact to share the gospel to them. I stop and listen and any face I see in my mind or name that comes into my thoughts, I write as the answer. I may ask if there are any offenses or anyone I need to forgive. I listen and do the same. I ask Him to reveal any sinful thoughts, actions or words. I do not argue with the answer. I confess and repent instead. It is talking and listening.

Look at the passage Jesus used again.

But you, when you pray, go into your inner room, close your door and pray to your Father who is in secret, and your Father who sees what is done in secret will reward you. And when you are praying, do not use meaningless repetition as the Gentiles do, for they suppose that they will be heard for their many words. So do not be like them; for your Father knows what you need before you ask Him. Pray, then, in this way: Our Father who is in heaven, Hallowed be Your name. Your kingdom come. Your will be done, on earth as it is in heaven. Give us this day our daily bread. And forgive us our debts, as we also have forgiven our debtors. And do not lead us into temptation, but deliver us from evil. For Yours is the kingdom and the power and the glory forever. Amen.

God said our prayer is to be between the Father and us. It is to be simple with no meaningless repetition such as "Father, God, blah blah Father God blah blah, I pray, blah blah, Father I pray, blah blah." You do not talk that way to anyone else, so why to God? Prayer is not more efficient because we complicate it. The exact opposite is true. The rest of the prayer shows us every area of our life is open to talking to God. The bottom line is we understand our lives are here for His glory and His Kingdom, and our prayer reflects that desire.

My working definition of prayer is this.

Prayer is communicating and cooperating with God to accomplish His will for His glory.

Prayer is communicating: It is just that. I talk to and listen to my Father. It is the same type of communication I have in my human, earthly relationships. I do not need a special vocabulary. I do not have to assume some form of religiosity. I talk to God. I listen to God.

Rejoice always; pray without ceasing; in everything give thanks; for this is God's will for you in Christ Jesus. (1 Thessalonians 5.16-18)

Rejoice in the Lord always; again I will say, rejoice! Let your gentle spirit be known to all men. The Lord is near. Be anxious for nothing, but in everything by prayer and supplication with thanksgiving let your requests be made known to God. And the peace of God, which surpasses all comprehension, will guard your hearts and your minds in Christ Jesus. (Philippians 4:4-7)

Devote yourselves to prayer, keeping alert in it with an attitude of thanksgiving; (Colossians 4:2)

Do you see prayer is something we do not only in our 'quiet time' but all the time? We are to always be open to the truth that God is Present, and He is at work in and around us. Through prayer, we acknowledge the Person and Presence of God in this moment. God says "I am right here" and in our prayers we acknowledge His Presence.

Prayer is communicating and cooperating with God to accomplish His will for His glory: God is at work and our goal is for His Kingdom to come. When we pray for ourselves and for other people, we are working with God. His Holy Spirit reveals to us people and things to talk to Him about and seek His working in it. He uses our prayers to work. It is beyond our comprehension, but somehow the Father incorporates our prayers into His working and to do His will. My prayer is the will of God and it does the will of God. In the following prayers of Paul, notice the components of prayer flow from one to the other. There is no section on petition followed by confession, then intercession. It is a flowing conversation about others and God working in their lives.

For this reason also, since the day we heard of it, we have not ceased to pray for you and to ask that you may be filled with the knowledge of His will in all spiritual wisdom and understanding, so that you will walk in a manner worthy of the Lord, to please Him in all respects, bearing fruit in every good work and increasing in the knowledge of God; strengthened with all power, according to His glorious might, for the attaining of all steadfastness and patience; joyously giving thanks to the Father, who has qualified us to share in the inheritance of the saints in Light. (Colossians 1:9-12)

For this reason I bow my knees before the Father, from whom every family in heaven and on earth derives its name, that He would grant you, according to the riches of His glory, to be strengthened with power through His Spirit in the inner man, so that Christ may dwell in your hearts through faith; and that you, being rooted and grounded in love, may be able to comprehend with all the saints what is the breadth and length and height and depth, and to know the love of Christ which surpasses knowledge, that you may be filled up to all the fullness of God. Now to Him who is able to do far more abundantly beyond all that we ask or think, according to the power that works within us, to Him be the glory in the church and in Christ Jesus to all generations forever and ever. Amen. (Ephesians 3:14-21)

Paul asked others to pray for him in order for God to use him.

Praying at the same time for us as well, that God will open up to us a door for the word, so that we may speak forth the mystery of Christ, for which I have also been imprisoned; that I may make it clear in the way I ought to speak. (Colossians 4:3-4)

For I know that this will turn out for my deliverance through your prayers and the provision of the Spirit of Jesus Christ, (Philippians 1:19)

As in everything, the ultimate purpose of what we do is the glory of the Father.

Whatever you ask in My name, that will I do, so that the Father may be glorified in the Son. If you ask Me anything in My name, I will do it. (John 14:13-14)

The focus of prayer is the Presence and Person of Jesus Christ. It is not an action that we do. It is a Person we encounter.

FASTING

I write this while in Bolivia under quarantine. It is May 6, 2020 and CoVid 19 has raced around the world. Here in Bolivia, we have been under a quarantine since the seventeenth of March. Our quarantine is a little more intense than the "Shelter In Place" orders in the States. You cannot leave your home at all. The only exception is for one five-hour period a week, based upon the number of your national ID card. On a set time you can walk, they allow no vehicles to purchase all your supplies for the following week. Police and military patrol to enforce the law. Violators receive a huge fine and eight hours in jail followed by as much as two years in prison. I may leave my home on Monday mornings from 7 am until noon. Each Monday I walk a six-mile loop to the market and back. On the way back I carry around 50 pounds of food in my backpack. I have it good. I have money and a refrigerator to store food. I can purchase a week of food at one time. Others here in Bolivia and the world are not in the same situation. They work as day workers. Many get paid at the end of their day and buy their food for the next day on the way home. Others get paid weekly, but because of no electricity or refrigeration or even room to store food, they must buy their food daily. The problem they are facing is that they have not worked since March. They do not have money. They do not have food. They are hungry.

God has worked so that through a governmental permission to drive that a fellow minister has we have been able to purchase food for many of the hungry in our area. As I type this, we have fed over 500 people for two weeks and will feed another 1,000 in the next week. God is allowing us to meet the most basic need in His name.

When you hear of someone being hungry, it evokes feelings of empathy. We avoid hunger. We seek to help others avoid hunger. There are ministries throughout the world and NGO's with the sole vision of helping the hungry.

When was the last time that you were really hungry? I don't mean a little hungry or it was time to eat. When was the last time that you felt hunger in such a way that it was the most consuming drive in your life at the moment? Most likely the answer to those of you in the target market of this book is never. You have wanted to eat, and you enjoy eating, but you have never truly experienced hunger.

In our culture, food is more than a utilitarian consumption of energy. Food is an art and an entertainment. We have an entire cable television network, actually more than one devoted to eating. We have reality shows about eating. We have eating contests. The restaurant industry in the United States is a multi-billion-dollar industry. We eat at both formal and informal occasions. We eat to celebrate and to mourn. We eat.

The third discipline that Jesus mentioned is one in which we have little or no experience. I have asked this question in pastor's conferences on two different continents and to about 75 different pastors: "How many of you have fasted in the last month? How many in the last year? How many of you have taught your congregation about fasting and led them to fast?" Here are the answers. No one. No one. No one. In my personal experience I have never led a conference where a single pastor had fasted within the last month for spiritual discipline, nor have I had any pastor who has taught their church to fast. Yet, look back at what Jesus said.

Whenever you fast, do not put on a gloomy face as the hypocrites do, for they neglect their appearance so that they will be noticed by men when they are fasting. Truly I say to you, they have their reward in full. But you, when you fast, anoint your head and wash your face so that your fasting will not be noticed by men, but by your Father who is in secret; and your Father who sees what is done in secret will reward you. (Matthew 6:16-18)

Jesus did not say "If you fast". His assumption of His disciples is that they will fast at least often enough for Him to include it in His top three disciplines mentioned in the Sermon on the Mount.

Spiritual Disciplines are the Spirit-Led habits and activities that I do in order to know God better and love Him more.

This is true also for fasting. Fasting is a Spirit-led habit and/or activity that I do in order to know God better and love Him more. I emphasize that because there is a diet fad in the States that started in 2019 and is growing. It is intermediate fasting. Many people have discovered that they can use the practice of fasting to stop gaining or lose weight. It is basic. If you eat a lot over a lengthy period, you will gain weight. If you eat a little over time, you lose weight. People discovered engorging themselves three times a day results in obesity. The pendulum has swung and people are choosing to eat one small meal a day and then 'fast' until the next day. This is not a spiritual discipline in order to help us know God better and love Him more. It is a weight loss plan.

Spiritual fasting is not to gain physical benefits. It is a way for us to take our minds off of the immediate need of our body and focus on our Lord. I use the term 'prayer trigger'. I fast to connect with Who God Is and what He is doing. When it is time for me to eat or whenever I feel hunger, I consider it a trigger to send me into the Presence of God. It reminds me of Who He is or the reason that I have chosen to fast.

Fasting is choosing to not eat in order to focus on the Person and Work of God.

Fasting is choosing to not eat. This definition is as simple as it gets and is self-explanatory. I want to stress that Biblically fasting is the abstinence of food. It is a pet peeve of mine when

I see people say, "I am going to fast from social media." or "I am fasting from television". This is nothing more than a self-denial of some activity. You may have a spiritual reason. God may have even led you to do it. Denying yourself a pleasure or some other activity is not a fast in the Biblical sense. Fasting denies ourselves food for a spiritual purpose. The thing I do not understand about our lack of fasting is that it is a discipline seen by God's people through the Scripture and church history.

Jesus, our example, fasted.

Then Jesus was led up by the Spirit into the wilderness to be tempted by the devil. And after He had fasted forty days and forty nights, He then became hungry. (Matthew 4:1-2)

Fasting is choosing to not eat in order to focus on the Person and Work of God. All throughout the Bible, God's people fasted. The discipline of fasting was used to show repentance and dependence upon God. People fasted to discern God's will. Fasting was a part of worship and focusing on God. It was used to humble oneself in the sight of God as you sought Him. Fasting is a discipline that transcends the Old and New Testaments. We see that Moses, Joshua, the Prophets, Jesus, John and his Disciples, Jesus' Disciples, Apostles, and early church leaders all practiced fasting.

Go, assemble all the Jews who are found in Susa, and fast for me; do not eat or drink for three days, night or day. I and my maidens also will fast in the same way. And thus I will go in to the king, which is not according to the law; and if I perish, I perish. (Ester 4:16)

They gathered to Mizpah, and drew water and poured it out before the Lord, and fasted on that day and said there, "We have sinned against the Lord." And Samuel judged the sons of Israel at Mizpah. (1 Samuel 7:6)

So I gave my attention to the Lord God to seek Him by prayer and supplications, with fasting, sackcloth and ashes. I prayed to the Lord my God and confessed and said, "Alas, O Lord, the great and awesome

God, who keeps His covenant and lovingkindness for those who love Him and keep His commandments, we have sinned, committed iniquity, acted wickedly and rebelled, even turning aside from Your commandments and ordinances. Moreover, we have not listened to Your servants the prophets, who spoke in Your name to our kings, our princes, our fathers and all the people of the land. (Daniel 9:3-6)

"Yet even now," declares the Lord, "Return to Me with all your heart, and with fasting, weeping and mourning; (Joel 2:12)

Now there were at Antioch, in the church that was there, prophets and teachers: Barnabas, and Simeon who was called Niger, and Lucius of Cyrene, and Manaen who had been brought up with Herod the tetrarch, and Saul. While they were ministering to the Lord and fasting, the Holy Spirit said, "Set apart for Me Barnabas and Saul for the work to which I have called them." Then, when they had fasted and prayed and laid their hands on them, they sent them away. (Acts 13:1-3)

When they had appointed elders for them in every church, having prayed with fasting, they commended them to the Lord in whom they had believed. (Acts 14:23)

and then as a widow to the age of eighty-four. She never left the temple, serving night and day with fastings and prayers. (Luke 2:37)

But as for me, when they were sick, my clothing was sackcloth; I humbled my soul with fasting, and my prayer kept returning to my bosom. (Psalm 35:13)

Then I proclaimed a fast there at the river of Ahava, that we might humble ourselves before our God to seek from Him a safe journey for us, our little ones, and all our possessions. (Ezra 8:21)

Finally, it is plain in the Bible that Jesus expects His followers to fast.

John's disciples and the Pharisees were fasting; and they came and said to Him, "Why do John's disciples and the disciples of the Phari-

sees fast, but Your disciples do not fast?" And Jesus said to them, "While the bridegroom is with them, the attendants of the bridegroom cannot fast, can they? So long as they have the bridegroom with them, they cannot fast. But the days will come when the bridegroom is taken away from them, and then they will fast in that day. (Mark 2:18-20)

Whenever you fast, do not put on a gloomy face as the hypocrites do, for they neglect their appearance so that they will be noticed by men when they are fasting. Truly I say to you, they have their reward in full. But you, when you fast, anoint your head and wash your face so that your fasting will not be noticed by men, but by your Father who is in secret; and your Father who sees what is done in secret will reward you. (Matthew 6:16-18)

So, how do we fast? There are all kinds of questions around fasting. What makes up a fast? How long should you fast? Can you do a partial fast? The answer to these is simple. Fasting is a Spirit Led activity. You follow the Holy Spirit as He leads you on your fast. I believe that the normal fast in the Bible is one of food. There are examples where God supernaturally enabled someone to fast from water also, but that was a miracle. Typically, a fast would be a minimum of one day and a maximum of 40. Skipping one meal is not truly a fast.

Fasting is a means to focus on God, and to seek Him as He leads you. Let me share a few personal examples from our family. I am typing this and it was time to eat lunch with the family. They only set the table for four instead of six. I asked why and my 18-year-old and 17-year-old daughters are fasting for 36 hours as they pray for a request. I did not even know about it, but when I saw it I realized God had given me a perfect illustration. My wife and I fast regularly as part of normal spiritual disciplines. We will fast one or two days a week each month and more if God leads. Occasionally God has led us to do extended fasts. In times of tremendous change, we have done these long fasts to center on God and not our own desires. We moved from Denver to Virginia and then from Virginia to Bolivia. Before each of these moves, we fasted together for 21 days. Our purpose was to humble ourselves and cast all of our own desires upon the Lord so we could hear from Him. We spent meal times, both preparing and eating, in prayer and contemplation upon the Lord. On more than one occasion, God has led one of us to do a forty-day fast. During this long fast, we allow ourselves a glass of juice in the morning and another in the evening. Other than that, it is water only. These fasts have been Spirit led activities in order to know God better and love Him more. During prolonged fasting we can both testify that it heightens our sensitivity to our own selfishness and wrong desires. The result of these extended times of fasting is that we learn to depend more upon our Father and recognize the inherit weakness of our flesh.

I would recommend that if you have never fasted before or rarely fasted that you start off with a simple 24 hour one. I usually eat lunch on Sunday with my family and then will fast until dinner on Monday or Tuesday. It is a great way to start. The purpose of the fast is not to avoid food, it is to connect with God. After you do a few 1-2 day fasts seek the Lord on doing a longer one, maybe for a week to 10 days. As you fast always use the time that you would normally eat to pray, read the Scripture, contemplate on Him, or some other means of connecting and focusing on the Lord. Let the time you normally used to feed your body for the nourishment of your soul.

GOD REALLY DOES LOVE ME

I mentioned in an earlier chapter my musical taste is eclectic. I listen to various genres. However, the truth is, I gravitate back to the Classic Rock of the 70's and 80's. I also love me some Beatles. "All You Need Is Love, Love, Love Is All You Need." I have to admit I like the Beatles. It may not sound very Christian of me, but I have about 50 songs on my iPad and I listen to them so much when my daughter was three, she walked through the living room eating a strawberry and singing 'Strawberry Fills Forever' (her re-write of the classic). I like the Beatles, but I do not get my theology from them. That being said, I believe they hit the nail on the head with the head with this title. All we need is to know how much God loves us, to love Him back, and to love others with the same love. Can you 'Imagine' what it would be like if we stopped working 'Eight Days A Week' to get God to love us and in order to 'Feel Fine' and 'Get Back' to the relationship we had with Him 'Yesterday'? Okay, I could do this all day long (and unfortunately, I could do the same thing with the Bee Gees and Jimmy Buffet—what does that say about me?). My point is GOD LOVES YOU! When you realize how much God loves you, then you love God right back. After a short while, you can't keep the fact God loves you to yourself. You then realize God loves all those other people in your life in the same way He loves you. You will feel compelled to help them understand God's incredible love.

A few times in my life I have had to go to court. Fortunately, and by the grace of God, never as a defendant, but as a witness and/or friend of a defendant. One time I was a witness, and in this case, they had required me to present my proof of identity before testifying. I stated who I was, and the attorney pointed out they had my birth certificate and driver's license on hand as proof. I never had to testify to my identity again. I stated once it and entered into evidence. At the end of the trial, the judge made his declaration as to the guilt of my friend and hit the gavel. The case was closed.

You and I see this all the time on television shows about law and lawyers. My favorite show for a while was Boston Legal. It was a show with a liberal slant, but superb writing. In these shows, and in reality, once something is proved, it is no longer up in the air. You don't have to keep entering the same thing into evidence. Imagine this scene:

Lawyer: For the record, state your name.
Me: Joe Holman
Lawyer: Do you have any proof of this?
Me: I have my birth certificate, passport, driver's license, fingerprints on file with the FBI, and my dental records all entered into evidence.
Lawyer: Your honor, I refer to all the above documents as proof of identity.
Judge: Let me see those...okay, these are legal proof, this is Joe Holman.

The case opens, and the Lawyer begins to ask me questions, but stops and this happens:

Lawyer: For the record, state your name.
Me: Joe Holman
Lawyer: Do you have any proof of this?
Me: I have my birth certificate, passport, driver's license, fingerprints on file with the FBI, and my dental records all entered into evidence.
Lawyer: Your honor, I refer to all the above documents as proof of identity.

Judge: Let me see those...okay, these are legal proof, this is Joe Holman.

Once established, the same dialogue begins.

Lawyer: For the record, state your name.

Me: I have my birth certificate, passport, driver's license, fingerprints on file with the FBI, and my dental records all entered into evidence.

Lawyer: Your honor, do you accept all the above documents as proof of identity?

Judge: Let me see those...okay, these are legal proof, this is Joe Holman.

The case proceeds again, but every three minutes the dialogue begins again. I am asked to prove my identity and give evidence to prove it. The judge accepts the proof, legally declares me on record as Joe Holman, and it repeats the cycle.

How much sense would this make? How much progress would take place in our legal or justice systems if nothing was ever truly proven? What does it take to establish something as 'proven' in our court system? Once something is declared proven, such as my identity, what would a judge do, in reality, if the lawyer kept trying to 're-open' my identity? Why do we do to God what not only makes no sense to us, but what we would never accept in our own courts?

Read that last question again. Here is what I mean. God has proven His love for us. It is established, legally and eternally. Yet, repeatedly, we declare it on trial. Let one adverse thing enter our lives, and we scream for a retrial. We call the previous court where God proved His love a facade. We put His love on trial again. And again. And again. Let us enter some sinful behavior, and we put His love on trial. Lose your job? God's love goes on trial. Bad health? God's love goes on trial. Broken relationship? God's love goes on trial. Earthquake, tsunami, hurricane, tornado, mudslide? God's love goes on trial. Act of war? God's love goes on trial.

When my son died last year, I had the unfortunate opportunity to be introduced via social media to a lot of other grieving parents. In some of these cases, there were Christian parents who had turned their back on God because their child died. One person was honest enough to put it into words. He said, "I no longer believe God loves me. If God loves me, why did He let my son die?"

This is what we do. We think God has to prove His love for us. In the present and future tense, God has to prove His love by doing whatever we deem needs to be done to prove it.

God does not have to prove His love. He has already, past tense, proven it. We want to declare a mistrial and try to get Him back into our court of circumstances.

By this the love of God was manifested in us, that God has sent His only begotten Son into the world so that we might live through Him. In this is love, not that we loved God, but that He loved us and sent His Son to be the propitiation for our sins.(1John 4:9-10)

Notice a couple of phrases. The first one is "By this". God points out something to us. He is saying an illustration has been given, proof has been established, and something has been shown. What is it? By this the love of God was manifested. Here is how we typically finish this sentence: 'By this the love of God was manifested to us, in that we have really good health. By this the love of God was manifested to us, our children grow up and are decent people. By this the love of God is manifested to us, the good-paying job with great security is given to you. By this is the love of God manifested to us, then list whatever good circumstances you want to list.

The opposite also happens. If the circumstances turn bad, we feel the phrase should be, "By this we do not know if God loves us. Usually we say it along these lines..."If God loves me, why would He..." The idea, especially among those of us who feel happiness is our right, is God owes us a good life. When you measure life by the amount of luxury you can experience, at least by your ability to live comfortably, when loving your children means giving them more than you had, anytime we don't receive the 'good life' from our heavenly Father, we assume we have done something wrong. If not that, then He is mad at us. Maybe He doesn't exist. I also think it is telling our doubts usually only occur when *our* lives are hurting. Rarely do we say, "If God really loves me, why are people hurting in South America?"

By this the love of God was manifested in us, that God has sent His only begotten Son into the world so that we might live through Him. In this is love, not that we loved God, but that He loved us and sent His Son to be the propitiation for our sins. (1John 4:9-10)

God manifested His love to us in this: He sent His only begotten Son into the world. God wanted us to see His love. So, He sent Jesus into the world so that we might live in Him. It says, "in this is love..." Once more, you do not see a lengthy list of grand life experiences to prove God's love. What you discover is He proved His love in the death of Jesus Christ. Jesus came into the world and died for our sins. Court has been called, the evidence given, and the judge has declared the case closed...God loves us.

Yet we don't believe this. We think the life, death, and resurrection of Jesus is only the first part of the chain of evidence. God sent Hs Son into the world to die for me. Now, I will admit that into evidence. However, there are a lot of other things we must consider, and my happiness is the most important. I will know God loves me because He sent Jesus into the world to give me the wonderful life. Where does the Bible teach this? How does this apply to people in communist China or North Korea?

Realizing God's love for us is not on trial revolutionized our lives. It allows us to face incredible odds and adversity. In 2004, my wife experienced a loss of memory. She became extremely anemic. Her initial blood work came back, and the Dr. said she had rare anomalies in her red blood cells. They were various sizes. They sent us to an oncologist. As part of the testing, she had an MRI and a Cat-scan. We also went to a neurologist. Our doctor was a friend of ours and pulled me aside. He said based on the preliminary testing; he wanted to prepare me for what looked like would happen. He felt all the indicators were pointing towards a brain tumor.

Later in the night, at the dinner table, we talked to our children. I told them mom appeared to be pretty sick. I asked them "How do we know God loves us?" My children were 15 and below. As they were thinking about it, I asked them again, "How do we know God loves us?" I continued, "Do we know God loves us because He will let mom live? Or do we know God loves us because He allowed Jesus to die?" Caleb, my 11-year-old replied, "We know He loves us because Jesus died for us."

My 11-year-old understood something billions of us struggle with. God does not prove His love by letting my wife outlive me. He does not have to prove His love by doing anything. He has ALREADY proven His love by sending His Son to die on the cross in my place. His love is not on trial. He proved His love. Yes, people get cancer...God proved His love at the cross, not in people staying healthy. Yes, people die. God proved His love at Calvary, not in people staying alive. Yes, really bad things happen to people and by people. God proved His love in the death of Jesus. All creation for all time can see His love at Calvary. He proved it. Past tense at Calvary. As a side note, my wife is okay. It was not a tumor. She is completely healthy. However, her being fine means nothing about God's love. He proved His love before my wife ever got sick, not by her health, but by Jesus paying the price of our sins.

The same thing happened when my son died. On Facebook I posted my circumstances do not determine my theology. God loves me. Period. My circumstances were horrible. God's love was constant. Before my son passed away, as I was asking people to pray, I posted this: **"God will not prove His love to me by my son living. He has already proved His love for me by His Son dying."**

Many of you can remember the first court room show. I am

not talking about Perry Mason. I mean the O.J. Simpson trial. They allowed cameras in the courtroom, and millions of people lost confidence in the American Judicial System. Who could forget the hard to fit glove? We watched as they called the witnesses to take the stand, as the State tried to prove its case, and as the defense destroyed argument after argument. Let me invite you back into a courtroom. Only this time it is not a fiasco. It is not even in the United States. It is not even in the world. It is outside of time and space. It is the Supreme Court of the Universe. God Himself is the Judge. On trial is the love of God, and all of creation is watching as the Devil tries to disprove God's love for His people. This is the exact scene of Romans 8. God has used Paul to establish His love for us in Christ. This love is so foreign, so hard to understand or believe, God knows we will meet it with skepticism. People will not believe God will forgive them, restore them, and redeem them because He loves them. They know the blackness of their hearts, and the darkness of creation.

So, God calls for a trial. The devil will present his case and prove to us God may love us, but His love is conditional. That is all he has to do. If God's love is conditional, we are in serious trouble. Does God love us? Or does God love us "IF"? We believe God loves us...IF. If we meet His demands. If we follow His rules. If we don't sin. If we go to church, read our Bibles, pray and try to get others to be like us. IF we vote for a certain political party. If we follow a system of morality. IF we...

The problem is, we can never meet the "IF of the conditional love of God. We always fail. One of the greatest lies of Satan is God's love is conditional upon some IF. This lie is not new, and in Romans 8 we see it defeated.

So, join me in the courtroom. Look around and see the twisted faces of demons, the hatred of sin, and the black-souled eyes of the fallen angel himself. Look at the witnesses lined up, ready to testify to the conditionality of God's love. The devil approaches the bench and calls his first witness.

*Who will separate us from the love of Christ? Will **tribulation**, or distress, or persecution, or famine, or nakedness, or peril, or sword? (Rom 8:35)*

The first witness called to the stand is Tribulation. He testifies. Tribulation talks about all the pain people experience in life. He goes back to the first sin, to the family of Adam, to the murder of a brother by a brother. He shows how people have always suffered hardship in a hard world. Over and over, throughout history, he plays scenes of sorrow. His testimony stops two or three times because he simply cannot speak through the tears. The courtroom is full of people who are nodding their head in agreement. There is a projector screen set up, and we watch actual scenes of earthquakes, volcanoes, floods (including the big one) and fires. After hours of testimony, the Devil stops asking questions and turns to the camera with a smug look. He stares into the lens and calls for his next witness.

*Who will separate us from the love of Christ? Will tribulation, or **distress**, or persecution, or famine, or nakedness, or peril, or sword? (Rom 8:35)*

Distress is the twin of Tribulation. He joins in where the testimony of Tribulation stopped. He goes back over some examples and paints a picture from the inside. Not only does tribulation happen to us, it happens in us. We don't experience tribulation on the news. We experience it in our hearts. It overwhelms us from the inside. Distress takes the formula of pain given to us by tribulation and makes it exponential. It makes it personal. It makes us own it. How can God really love us? Tribulation and Distress have made a solid case against it. The devil is not finished.

*Who will separate us from the love of Christ? Will tribulation, or distress, or **persecution**, or famine, or nakedness, or peril, or sword? (Rom 8:35)*

The devil stands up and shouts the famous philosophical argument."If God is all-powerful, then He could have prevented or stopped any of these events from taking place! Why didn't He? Because He DOESN'T CARE! If He truly loved you, then why would He let you suffer and die...not only suffer and die, but be TARGETED for death because you are His child. Shouldn't the opposite happen? If I love my child, I wouldn't put them in harm's way. I don't watch them suffer. I don't allow people to hurt them, let alone torture and kill them. Why does God allow this? He DOESN'T LOVE YOU."

The devil isn't finished. He turns from active hostility to the passive lack of interest God has for His children. It looks like He really did wind up the universal clock and walk away.

*Who will separate us from the love of Christ? Will tribulation, or distress, or persecution, or **famine**, or **nakedness**, or peril, or sword? (Rom 8:35)*

God has been watching, but has He been caring? This is the question the devil wants to know as he catalogues all the suffering brought upon people throughout time by 'natural' causes. Even modern-day insurance policies recognize the complacency of God through their 'act of God' stipulations. How can we honestly believe God loves us when He allows these things to happen to us?

What is God's answer to this first barrage of accusations? How does He refute such powerful evidence? God the Father raises His hand and points to His Son. He points to how Jesus stepped into time and went to the cross. This not only establishes His love, but it puts these things into a unique perspective. Watch what God does.

But in all these things we overwhelmingly conquer through Him who loved us. (Rom 8:37)

God does not refute the damage. He doesn't seek to defend

Himself. He doesn't minimize what the devil has said. Instead, He points to the eternal end. Yes, this life can be hard. However, in the divine workings of God, the most horrible event we can experience is put together for our good. We do not endure these things. We are not suffering victims of life. We are warriors. We are conquering warriors. We are more than conquerors. We are not victims; we are victors. How? We are victorious through Him who loved us. God's love for us rewrites the tragedy of life into a symphony of love. He may allow dreadful things to happen to us. Suffering doesn't mean He does not love us. He gave His love to us through Jesus. What it means is because we know He loves us, we can challenge and overcome the highest obstacle of the enemy or of a fallen world. Death himself has lost his ability to threaten us.

God takes the offensive. He goes through a laundry list of potential witnesses who are waiting to be put on the stand. Is there anyone that can separate us from God's love?

For I am convinced that neither death, nor life, nor angels, nor principalities, nor things present, nor things to come, nor powers, nor height, nor depth, nor any other created thing, will be able to separate us from the love of God, which is in Christ Jesus our Lord. (Romans 8:38-39)

For I am convinced that neither **death.** The most obvious challenger is death. We have feared death since Adam took the fruit and was expelled from the Garden. Death has been personified and vilified. It is the door we all must walk through, and the one we fear the most. If anything can end God's love for us, it must be death. So, God begins with the greatest enemy and defeats him at the cross. His love for us is greater than death.

For I am convinced that neither death, nor **life** Then, what is the opposite of death? It is life. It could be there is something in this life I can do, or can be done to me, that can pull me away from God's love? Nope. Life, and all the beings who possess life, are powerless.

For I am convinced that neither death, nor life, nor **angels***.*.The word powerless makes me think of powerful. The most powerful beings ever created are the angels. In the Scripture we find one angel could slaughter 185,000 soldiers in one night. Angels are far beyond our ability. So, if an angel, say Michael the archangel, wanted to come between me and the love of God, I would not have a chance. No, the fact is the angel has no chance. Not even an angel can push God away from me.

For I am convinced that neither death, nor life, nor angels, nor **principalities***,* Okay, Michael cannot divide me from God's love, but what about Satan? Angels might hold the power but not have the desire. That is why they cannot separate me from God...they would never want to. But demons? Demons are fallen angels. They posses all the power of angels but hate me with a hatred I cannot understand. Satan wants to kill me. He wants to destroy me. Hostility towards me consumes him. He desires my eternal damnation with him in the lake of fire. He, if nothing or no one else, surely HE can make God stop loving me. Nope. Look at the list. The word 'principalities" is referring to supernatural and demonic power. Satan has lost, and the cross has proved it.

For I am convinced that neither death, nor life, nor angels, nor principalities, nor **things present***,* Life, death, angels and principalities are all abstract thugs from beyond time. They are theoretical. I want something concrete. Look around at life. Look at all the horrible events, at the selfishness of humanity, at the suffering imposed upon others, and at the destructive power of nature. We think if you or I could scour the earth, the galaxy, or the universe, we would come across something undiscovered but capable of pulling me out of the hand of God. God tells us we could go anywhere and there is NOTHING in the present makes God love us less than He has in the past.

For I am convinced that neither death, nor life, nor angels, nor principalities, nor things present, **nor things to come,** God expands His perspective. He lets us know all the events of the past, and all the beings of the present including the supernatural, cannot lessen His love for us. But what about the unknown? The past can be analyzed, and the present experienced, but who knows what the future might bring? I have a vivid imagination, and I can envision a future in which God stops loving me. I will commit some sin or do something so bad...maybe not today but in 10 or 15 years or even longer, but I could do something that would cause God to turn His back on me. In the future, there could be a new perversion of nature that rises up and plucks me from His care. God, Who knows the future with the same certainty He knows the past; God, who has written the future, tells me there is nothing that could ever threaten His love for me.

For I am convinced that neither death, nor life, nor angels, nor principalities, nor things present, nor things to come, nor powers, **nor height, nor depth, nor any other created thing, will be able to separate us from the love of God,** *which is in Christ Jesus our Lord. (Romans 8:38-39)* My Father has not finished. He says we could go up for all eternity, turn around and go down for all eternity, and find there is not anything in all of creation that will separate us from the love of God which is in Christ Jesus.

The courtroom is silent for a moment, and then billions of uncountable creation praise Him. He proved His case. His Son is all the evidence He need provide. He loves us.

This courtroom scene is not an extrapolation of a passage by a preacher. It is a vital truth foundational to so many other things. God loves me. He has proven it. As we told my children, He does not prove He loves us by the circumstances of our lives. He HAS PROVEN He loves us by His death. There is no need for any more proof. He loves us. His love is unconditional. There is nothing we can do to increase it, decrease it, or change it. He loves us in Christ, forever.

Why spend so much time and energy seeking to teach this truth? Because we do not really believe it. I was teaching an adult Bible study class in my church when I pastored. This church is a doctrinally sound church. It is full of mature, Bible knowing Christians. I would rank it high among churches all across the world for the theology and doctrine the people possess. However, as I taught the unconditional love of God to these mature Christians, they struggled with it. It was difficult to come to terms with the fact God loves me, period....not God loves me if/when, but period. It is difficult to believe this truth. We say it, but when pushed on it, we don't think it is true.

Therefore, many churches/Christians believe a believer can lose their salvation. They believe God loves them if and only if they keep the list. The list varies, we must keep it. It might be read your Bible, pray, go to church and try to get other people to... It might be some moral or list of ethics. It might be a religious activity list. Whatever it is, we believe failing to keep this list results in a lack of spiritual growth which ultimately can lead to a forfeiture of eternal life. So we scream at people who try to take away our lists.

People have called me a heretic because I teach once God saves us, we are saved. We are saved from everyone and everything, including ourselves. I teach we cannot ever, in the past, present or future, separate ourselves from God's love in Christ. I point them to this list and show no matter what we do; it falls under the category of things present or of any created thing. Yet, we do not believe it. My church, during the discussion time, had a lot of "what if; what about, but..." type of questions. There was so much doubt that what began as an introduction to a 45 minute Sunday School class ended up being a six-week course in God's love and a sermon series.

We don't understand. We don't have to. We are told to believe it. The Bible teaches God loves us with an unconditional, eternal, never-ending and never changing love. It is a love is beyond our knowledge, so we move into the realm of faith. We by faith know the love is beyond knowledge. Faith in Him permits us to believe He loves even us, revolutionizes our lives.

KNOWN BY OUR LOVE

When I was in Highschool, I had friends who were in track. I tried to be. I was even on the track team when I was a freshman. I ran the 880. I have what may be a record in the State of Texas. I came in last (not second to last, not near the back-- LAST) in every single race. I tell my kids that even before I knew Christ, I took part in a ministry of making people feel better about themselves. I was the person who made second-to-last possible. I totally stunk at track. I was also pretty bad at baseball, not good at basketball, third string in football and mediocre in tennis. As I evaluate my high school sports record, I ask myself why I was in sports. I figured this out my senior year and played nothing. I marvel it took me that long to admit that I was pathetic. However, I was in sports and that allowed me to have friends in sports. One of my friends in track was good at the high jump and at pole vaulting. Occasionally a few of us would get together and just practice jumping. It was straightforward. You had three tries to clear the bar. If you cleared it, then you raised it another inch. This kept going until you could no longer clear the bar. Your goal was to keep raising the bar. It was a noble goal for me, because I cannot jump over a sheet of notebook paper.

There is something in the Bible that will make you feel you are me looking up at an 18' pole vault bar with the challenge of high jumping it. A truth that is simply beyond our ability, yet it is our responsibility.

Go back to the love of God. Remember what we have discovered. God's love for His children is unconditional. It has NO CONDITIONS. Therefore, nothing can separate us from the love of God. It is freely and completely given to us by Him with no condition at all being put upon it or us. If it had only one condition...even a tiny one, then it would not be unconditional and it would be possible to be separated from it.

Let me explain it in a way that I have used in marriage counseling and in premarital counseling. I first used this when a couple came to me because the wife had committed adultery. The wife had come to the husband and confessed the sexual sin after being convicted by the Holy Spirit and repenting of it. The husband wanted a divorce. As I talked to them, it soon became obvious (as it always does) that the adultery was just a huge sin (you understand what I mean by this) in a history of sins linked together. It also became clear (as it almost always does) that the husband had failed his wife in many areas. He had not committed adultery, but neither had he loved her as Christ loved the church. I explained God's love to them. I pointed out how God loved the husband. I took him to Bible passages that revealed God's love for him during his own sin, and in spite of it. I had him confess that he believed God had loved him in eternity past and would continue to love Him without even the tiniest condition throughout all time.

He believed this and was thankful for it. Let me take you into my office that day.

"So, you see God loves you? That He loves you in Christ, and that His love for you is unconditional?" I asked him.

"Yes."

I continued, "If you were to sin, would God love you less than He does right now? Or if you were to do some super Christian thing like go to the mission field, would it make God love you more than this moment?"

"No. God loves me unconditionally. But what does this have to do with us?" He wanted to know.

"Let's look at a passage of Scripture together. Ephesians 5 says this: 'Husbands, love your wives as Christ loved the church.' 1 Peter tells us we are to love our wives 'in the same way' that Jesus loves us." I explained to him. He could see where I was going with this principle, but the illustration that I used rocked his world.

It was so powerful that I have used it several times in marriage conferences to illustrate God's unconditional love.

"If you love your wife unconditionally like Jesus loves you, that means that you will love her just as much when she is in bed with another man as you do when she is having sex with you."

Our conversation continued.

"I will not love my wife if she has sex with another man.", he insisted.

"Okay. I can see your point. You will love your wife on one condition. She must agree to never have sex with him again."

"Yes."

"So, she agrees to never have sex with him, but she really wants to have sex with him. Is that okay?"

"No! She cannot want to have sex with him! She must not even see him."

"Okay, let's write this down. You have three conditions that I think anyone would agree with. She cannot have sex with him. She cannot want to have sex with him. She cannot see him."

"So, she just emails him, goes to chat rooms with him, and talks to him on the phone. Is that good enough for you?" He expanded his list to include the prohibition of these items and we summarized it up by a total lack of contact of any kind...the list grew. It also incorporated emotions and desires.

"Now, our list is at about 10 items. Not that big of a deal. But I just thought of something. What if it isn't this guy, but another co-worker that she wants to have sex with?"

The list included all co-workers and all lustful thinking. It included all non-work contact with any other man. It grew to cover her internet browsing and her movie and television choices. By now, he saw that his one condition was not one condition.

"Here is the thing." I said, "There are only two types of love. We either love like God does unconditionally; or we love like people do and put conditions on our love. What does God want us to do?"

What he realized that day, and what I think we all soon realize for ourselves, is that unconditional love is a great thing to receive, but when it comes to giving it, the bar is pretty high. Jesus even referred to this in Luke 6 by saying that children of the Kingdom are to love others who don't love us, who abuse and misuse us, and who hurt us. If we only love the ones who love us, how is that any different than sinners?

I am talking about raising the bar. Let's see how high God has actually raised it.

The Father loves us. How does He love us? What is the type of love He has for us?

Just as the Father has loved Me, I have also loved you; abide in My love. (John 15:9)

I in them and You in Me, that they may be perfected in unity, so that the world may know that You sent Me, and loved them, even as You have loved Me. (John 17:23)

and I have made Your name known to them, and will make it known, so that the love with which You loved Me may be in them, and I in them." (John 17:26)

Imagine if you can, and we can't, but try to imagine how the Father loves the Son. Picture the passion, the emotion, the unbroken direction of His heart. God the Father loves God the Son with pure, perfect love.

Now, let your imagination go even farther than this. God the Father says that He loves YOU the same way, in the same manner, and with the same love that He has for the Son! The Father loves us like He loves Jesus. It is not just in the same way, but with the SAME LOVE. God loves His children with the same love that He loves His Son! Wow! It gets even more profound.

A new commandment I give to you, that you love one another, even as I have loved you, that you also love one another. (John 13:34)

This is My commandment, that you love one another, just as I have loved you. (John 15:12)

Therefore be imitators of God, as beloved children; and walk in love, just as Christ also loved you and gave Himself up for us, an offering and a sacrifice to God as a fragrant aroma. (Ephesians 5:1-2)

Husbands, love your wives, just as Christ also loved the church and gave Himself up for her (Ephesians 5:25)

Do not let this pass you by. Follow the line of thought and raise your bar.

God the Father loves me 'just as' and with the 'same love' that He loves the Son.

Jesus Christ the Son loves me with the 'same love' and 'just as' the Father loves Him.

I am then told that I am to love other people 'just as' Jesus loves me.

I am to love other people the way that Jesus loves me.

Jesus loves me the way the Father loves Him.

Therefore, I am to love other people the way that the Father loves the Son!

This is why the world will know we are His disciples by our love. It is because our love is the love of God! It is heavenly, unconditional love. It is love not based on the worth, the merit, or the actions of the one receiving it. It is the love of the Father.

Imagine a world in which husbands loved their wives like this. Can you see what would happen if we loved gays, Muslims, and pagans like this? What if we loved people that hated us just like we loved those that love us, without condition? What would happen in the church if we started loving each other, then other denominations, then the lost, and then the world in the same way that the Father loves the Son? How about the church loving drug addicts and street people? Wouldn't it be transforming to the world if we really were known, not by our economic policies or by what we were against, but by our love? Is there anywhere in the Bible where we are told that the world will know that we are followers of Jesus by our political party?

I say that maybe, just maybe, if we raised the bar and said that we are to love others the way that Jesus loves us, just as the Father loved Him, then world missions would become a reality and the poor would receive help.

The bar is high. Let's be honest. It is too high for us to clear. It is like me in high school track. We cannot and will not do this. We are incapable. So, what do we do?

My wife loves Starbucks Frappuccino's. Since we live in Bolivia, she rarely gets them. One time, I was in a store, and they had them for sale. It was a month before Christmas, so I bought them all. I paid $3 a bottle for 143 bottles. It was the best Christmas present I have ever given to my wife. For the next several months, every morning she would wake up and one of our kids would bring her a frappuccino. My four-year-old daughter took one to her in the morning, and with all the pride of a young child helping mom said, "Mommy, I brought you a Crapucino". It was almost 10 years ago, and to this day we call them Crapucinos. When we are in the States, I tell the barista I would like a "Crapucino". I have never had one correct my pronunciation. We renamed the product.

This happened to love. It is a little different, because we have not only renamed but have also replaced the genuine thing. We have misunderstood what it means to love for so long we now believe our distortion of the truth is the truth. For example, if you look up a definition of the word, "love", in a dictionary you will find it wrapped in emotional or sexual terms. Love, it seems, is a pleasant feeling or good sex. Neither one of those are unconditional actions. Therefore, we don't understand how to love. We have redefined the term.

There is no doubt loving others is what God desires. Jesus, when asked what the most important command was, replied it was to love God and love others. We call this reply in Mark 12, the great commandment. God commands us to love Him with all we are, and to love our neighbor as we would love our very own beings. The Bible expands this command at various places to where we are to love our neighbor, our Christian brothers and sisters, our wives and husbands, our children and the final kicker, even our enemies. It is when we love our enemies people can tell we are different.

Earlier, I talked how important it was to have a target. We need to aim for something. As the old saying goes, "If you aim at nothing, you will hit it every time." So, what is the goal, the target of the teaching ministry of the church? What is it we are aiming at when we stand in our pulpits, behind our lectures, or in our classes? If you continue looking at what God has to say, you discover loving others is the goal of not only our lives, but the church itself. As a pastor, my purpose is to teach people to love God and love others. Look at what the Holy Spirit inspired the Apostle Paul to write as the aim of the Christian teacher in 1 Timothy 1:5. *"The goal of our instruction is love..."* Paul said the principal aim of the teaching ministry of the church was to teach people how to love. I believe this so much, that in the early 90s after a time of fasting and praying, I developed a life mission statement. The first part of my statement declares:

"My purpose is to help people know God better and love Him more."

God expands this teaching on in the famous chapter on love, 1 Corinthians 13. In the first view verses we learn loving others is such a chief priority that if we do not have love, nothing else we do matters.

If I speak with the tongues of men and of angels, but do not have love,

I have become a noisy gong or a clanging cymbal. If I have the gift of prophecy, and know all mysteries and all knowledge; and if I have all faith, so as to remove mountains, but do not have love, I am nothing. And if I give all my possessions to feed the poor, and if I surrender my body to be burned, but do not have love, it profits me nothing. (1 Corinthians 13:1-3)

Without love, all we say is a loud noise. Without love, we waste all of our spiritual gifts. Without love, all of our knowledge is ignorance. Without love, all of our faith and all of our sacrifices are worthless. Without love I do nothing, accomplish nothing, and am nothing. Love is not merely an emotion, it is the foundation of all other virtues and actions.

Love is not an emotion, it is an active force in our lives. It changes me.

Love is patient, love is kind and is not jealous; love does not brag and is not arrogant, does not act unbecomingly; it does not seek its own, is not provoked, does not take into account a wrong suffered, does not rejoice in unrighteousness, but rejoices with the truth; bears all things, believes all things, hopes all things, endures all things. (1 Corinthians 13:4-7)

Look at 1 Corinthians 13:4-7. In the early part of my Christian journey, and my ministry, I always viewed this as a "to-do list". I taught love is not something you feel, it is something you do. I loved to quote the platitude which said, "Love is a verb not a noun." I preached a series called "How To Be A Better Lover" based on this passage. My series was full of things to do. Love is patient. I therefore preached a four-point sermon on how to be patient. Love is kind. No worries, I have three steps to kindness. I did this throughout these verses. I had an entire sermon on each "love is" declaration. It was a great series. I loved it, and so did my church. I only wish it had been the teaching of the Bible.

This is not a "To-Do List". It is a checklist. I am called to love others unconditionally. How do I know if I am loving this way? If I am, then I will be kind and forgiving. See the difference? If this is a to-do list, then being kind produces love. If this is a checklist, then being kind reveals love, or the lack of it.   The first idea is patience causes love. The second is it is the effect of love. This understanding makes all the difference in the world. Love is not something you feel, it is something you do, but there is a caveat.

One time I got angry at my son. He had disobeyed an understood house rule and had done it on purpose. I confronted him. During the confrontation things escalated, and I responded with angry words, a loud voice and a punishment disproportionate to the crime. I went to him about an hour later, after the Holy Spirit had worked in my heart. Here is what I said.

"Son, I need you to forgive me. Earlier I got angry, and I yelled at you. I abused my authority and declared an unjust punishment. This was not because of what you had done. My anger was not in response to you. I need you to forgive me, because the Bible teaches love is not easily angered. God tells us love does not keep a record of wrongs. I did both. When I punished you, I was not loving you with God's love. Will you please forgive me for my unloving attitude?"

Let me explain. My son was in full-blown teenager mode. It was the huffing, puffing, eye-rolling, self-defending and rule attacking setting. He was argumentative and disrespectful. None of that matters. My love is to be proactive and from my heart. It is not the result of his actions. When I evaluated my behavior, the checklist did not reveal the love of God. Even during correcting teenage rebellion, the love of God is still patient and kind. I did not see the love of God. I saw the fickle love of Joe, which depends on being well received to continue being given. This checklist is a way for us to see our own walk with Christ. Jesus died for me because I am the type of man that would yell at a juvenile son for behaving like a child. I need Jesus. I need the gospel. I can see that when I test my love life by this checklist. I don't need love that is a product of my effort. This is the exact opposite of the gospel message. It is not effort. It is grace. I need grace-love.

This is where we redefine the terms and leave our Crapucino love for the genuine thing. What I am about to explain in my next two points is life changing. I know because it changed my life. This is something pastors say a lot, and most of the time it is hyperbole or an outright exaggeration. Here, it is truth.

Love is a verb. Love is something you do. Love is action. That is what 1 Corinthians 13:1-7 teach us. Love influences and changes. Love produces action. However, the phrase I used to 'love' to say, "Love is a verb, not a noun" is not true. Love is also a noun.

Love is not only something I do, it is something I receive.

Love is a product. I am the receiving agent of a product called love.

Beloved, let us love one another, for love is from God; and everyone who loves is born of God and knows God. (1 John 4:7)

In the first part of this verse, we see love is action. We are to love one another. However, there is a key part of this verse that is often overlooked. *Love is from God.* The love in our lives that influences and changes us and allows us to love others in a way that shows know God is something from God. It is something He gives us.

But the fruit of the Spirit is love, joy, peace, patience, kindness, goodness, faithfulness (Galatians 5:22)

This famous passage contrasts the works of the flesh with the fruit of the Spirit. We will dive into this in the next lesson, but the point is the fruits of the Spirit are something we receive from God. As we abide in the Holy Spirit, and He fills us, God gives us Spiritual Fruit. One of those fruits is love. Just as an additional push towards understanding love does come from God, look at a couple of those other fruits and you see 1 Corinthians lists them where God describes love. Love is a product of the Holy Spirit. It is something the Holy Spirit gives us.

When I am teaching on this aspect, I like to use a tangible illustration. I will ask someone in the audience to bring me something. It might be a chair, or a lectern, or something there near the stage and in sight. When they bring it, I ask them everything about it. How was it made? What type of materials did they use? How long did it take them to make it? I ask question after question about the manufacturing process until their inability to answer frustrates them. I point out all of my questions were moot. It was not their task to manufacture the product. All they needed to do was deliver the product.

When we are in the States, we take full advantage of Amazon and other mailing services. We buy virtually every non-consumable product online. After we buy it, they deliver it to our home. For example, I purchased a new laptop. I eagerly waited for it. One day about a week later, a brown truck pulled into my driveway. Do you know what the driver did? Do you think he pulled into my driveway and opened up a box of tools and supplies? Imagine him with a circuit board and a soldering iron dutifully connecting the various parts of the laptop in his truck. He finishes manufacturing of my laptop and hands it to me before driving to the next home and building a diffuser for essential oils in their driveway.

That is not what happens. The driver is not the manufacturer. It is not his job to create or make anything. His job is simple. He is to deliver a product. The box has an address on it. He takes the box to the address and gives it to the person on the label.

For too long we have confused our role. We look at love as something we manufacture. We have even changed the name of sex and call it "lovemaking". We look at all the people in our lives and try to manufacture the love they need.

Here is the crux of the issue. God has commanded us to love others unconditionally with His Love. We try to love others unconditionally with our love. The love of Joe is not unconditional. So, since I cannot love unconditionally with my love, I give up trying and love others with a cheap religious imitation which always results in some conditions being placed upon it. It is not the love of Joe others need. That love I can do. The love of Joe yells at disobedient kids on the journey to maturity. The love of Joe ignores the homeless man with the sign at the traffic signal. Joe's love is religiously, ethnically and socio-economically based. My love is so pathetic.

God commanded us to love others with His Love. I do not manufacture His love. God did not give us the ability to make His love. Stay with me on this. I cannot make God's love, but I can possess it. I can receive it and give it. I cannot make it.

So, how can I love others with God's love if I cannot manufacture God's love? I do it by receiving it from Him. It is a fruit of the Holy Spirit. God wants to love my son (or wife, or the clerk at the store, or my enemy, etc.). He gives me His love and tells me to deliver it to the other person. I am not called to manufacture His love, no more than the UPS driver builds a computer in my driveway. I am called to deliver His love. God has His love with the address of my wife written on the label. I am to pick up His love from Him and deliver it to my wife. In the same way UPS delivers a package to your doorstep, you are to deliver God's love to other people. You receive it from God. You take it to others. I don't have to try to pretend my love is unconditional because it is not. However, I can receive God's unconditional love and take it to others.

I will explain this in more detail in the next chapter, but the summary form is, as I abide in the Spirit and walk in Him, He produces or gives me His fruit. One of the fruits He produces is Love. He also gives me Kindness and Patience among other virtues. As I evaluate how I treat other people, if I do not see the fruit of Love being manifested in my life (the checklist), then I can know at this moment I am not abiding in Christ. If I were abiding in Him, I would bear much fruit. My lack of fruit is the proof I am not abiding. My anger did not reveal the sin of my son. It revealed the sin of my heart. God's love for my child did not vacillate based upon the behavior of my son. It was steadfast.

My love changed, and the change revealed my need for Christ. Love is a noun. Love is not just something I do; it is something I receive.

One more vital thing to understand about love.

Love is not just something I do; it is something I receive.

Love is not just something I receive; it is Someone I am with.

My favorite movie series of all time is the Star Wars world. I remember watching the first one, Episode IV, over ten times when I was in High School. I saw every one of them, to this present day and the spinoff and backstory movies, on opening day. It is a family tradition to be there. My daughters have even had their photos taken on the red carpet with the real R2D2! We love Star Wars. One thing we must avoid, however, is allowing movie theology to affect our own worldview. This has happened in a small way with love. Christians view love as a 'force'. I even own a collection of songs and the title of the cd is "The Power Of Love". We think love is this impersonal attribute or virtue which causes change. This is not true.

Love is a Person.

The one who does not love does not know God, for <u>God is love</u>. (1 John 4:8)

We have come to know and have believed the love which God has for us. <u>God is love</u>, and the one who abides in love abides in God, and God abides in him. (1 John 4:16)

Two times God makes a powerful statement. He says, "God is love."

One thing we will see over and over in this book on discipleship is this: **It is all about God**. Over and over, we will come back to the heart of the gospel. God wants to have a love relationship with me, and He has done everything possible to do so. He loves me. My life is complete in Him. Not in doing what He says, but in

HIM. Love is the same thing. He is the focus.

Let me put the lesson together for you.

God is love. I am to focus on Him. I confess my sins and make sure my heart is pure as I abide, live and walk in Him. As I am with Him, I understand and see things from His perspective. I realize the importance of love and His call for me to love others with His love.

While I am abiding in Him and becoming more like Him through the ministry of the Holy Spirit, I receive the fruits of the Spirit in my life. The Holy Spirit gives me the fruit of love. The fruit of the Holy Spirit works in my life and I have His love, patience, kindness, etc. I am changed by His love.

I, through Him, understand His love is not only for me. I am to be a conduit of His love and give His love to others. I can deliver the unconditional love of God to the people in my life. It is no longer the love of Joe. It is His Presence, His Spirit, and His love in me. I can love others unconditionally because I am not doing it. He is doing it in me and through me.

One day I came home from the office and to be honest I had experienced a very trying day. In the ministry there are some days where people are not nice to their pastor. There are days that just push those of us who are in full-time ministry to the limits. This was one of those days. When I pulled into my drive-way, the trashcans were still at the road and one was knocked over. The kids know they are supposed to get the cans at lunch and put them back in the garage. As I pulled up, I had to stop and get a bicycle out of the way so I could pull into the garage itself. I walked into the house, and I was ready to transfer my nasty day to other people. I said something, I cannot remember what, to my wife in a snippy manner. She answered me and a few moments later I was rude again. The third time she turned to me and I was hoping to get the response I had been pushing for. Instead, she looked into my eyes and said, "Babe, I can see you have had a bad day. You seem upset." She walked over and took me into an enormous hug. After about 30 seconds of silently hugging me, she said, "Is there anything I can do, any way I can serve you?" She destroyed my desire to be mean. Her fruit of patience, kindness, peace, gentleness and love overcame me.

When she tells her viewpoint, it includes her running to the cross six or seven times and asking Jesus to fill her with the Spirit so she could respond in a manner which would glorify Him and help me. She says she had to check her heart and have the Holy Spirit stop her words several times. She prayed for me. Her focus was not on the injustice of the moment and how I was treating her. She was looking at Jesus and what He wanted to do at the moment. This is a great example of what I am referring to. I was not in the kitchen with Denise. I was in the kitchen with God and Denise. He was fully present, and she knew it. His Person gave her through the Spirit the ability to perceive what was going on through His eyes and also His fruit. She then delivered His fruit to me.

We can live this scenario out in every relationship we have. We should live it out. This is how the world knows we are His disciples, by our love.

THINK RIGHT

When I gave my life to Christ, there was a radical change. I grew up rather rough. My father was an atheist, and he raised us to think lowly of religion. When I was 14, I started smoking marijuana and then graduated to other things as I aged. I became an immoral person.

Then, a year after I graduated High School, I met Jesus. He came in my life and I immediately started living differently. Within a few months, my friends called me either "Joe The Baptist" or "Preacher". I shared Christ with all of them. I attended church and joined a discipleship group. In college I would pass out tracts as I walked between classes and at night, I would go to the various hang out areas and witness to people. I stopped using drugs and drinking. I attended church. I listened only to Christian music. I stopped cussing. I totally changed all my behavior.

One day I was talking to my pastor and bragging. I told him of all the things that I no longer did and the things I was doing. I then said something that I remember as if it were yesterday.

I said, "I am doing all the right things. I just keep thinking of the wrong things. My actions are all good, but my thoughts aren't." I meant it in a good way. His answer is probably why I remember this conversation from almost forty years ago.

He said, "Joe, you are going about it the wrong way. You must change your thoughts. You need to transform your mind. If you think correctly, you will do what you need to do. Changing your actions but not your thoughts is a dangerous thing. Change your thoughts first. Your behaviors will follow."

I walked away from that meeting a little chastened and with

my pride hurt. However, it made me think. He had recommended a few books to me on the subject and I read them. Fast forward almost forty years and I wholeheartedly agree with him. You win or lose this life in the arena of your thoughts.

A disciple of Jesus must learn to think like Jesus thinks. If I think the right way, then my words will be the right words and my actions will be the right actions. It all starts in the mind. Let's look at a few passages. As we look at them, watch for words that reference your thought life. Words such as thoughts, mind, understanding, wisdom, and think to name a few. I will put them in bold as we come across them.

*Therefore I urge you, brethren, by the mercies of God, to present your bodies a living and holy sacrifice, acceptable to God, which is your spiritual service of worship. And do not be conformed to this world, but **be transformed by the renewing of your mind**, so that you may prove what the will of God is, that which is good and acceptable and perfect. For through the grace given to me I say to everyone among you not **to think** more highly of himself than he ought **to think**; but **to think** so as to have sound judgment, as God has allotted to each a measure of faith. (Romans 12:1-3)*

This is one of the more well-known passages. It is straightforward. We are to present bodies as a sacrifice to God. Much in line with the teaching the disciplines are spiritual and physical, notice that presenting our bodies is our spiritual service. As we present our bodies, it addresses one part in particular. We are to avoid being conformed to this world by renewing our mind. This is what my pastor was telling me forty years ago. I was changing my behavior. You do not modify your behavior; you renew your mind. As you renew your mind, you understand God's will for your life, which leads you to think of yourself correctly. It is mental.

*Be **anxious** for nothing, but in everything by prayer and supplication with thanksgiving let your requests be made known to God. And the* *peace of God, which surpasses all comprehension, will guard your hearts and your minds in Christ Jesus. Finally, brethren, whatever is true, whatever is honorable, whatever is right, whatever is pure, whatever is lovely, whatever is of good repute, if there is any excellence and if anything worthy of praise, dwell on these things. (Philippians 4:6-8)*

We are not to worry, which is to think negatively about life and uncertain futures. Instead, through prayer we trust God and His peace will guard not just our emotions, but our thoughts, our minds. God then gives us an imperative statement. It is a command to control our thought life. We are to dwell, to think about these things. I like how the Amplified Bible stresses the last part of this verse,

think continually on these things [center your mind on them, and implant them in your heart.

This was actually the first verse that I ever memorized. To this day, as I seek to offer my thoughts to God for His glory, I will go over this checklist. For example, my wife does something that I did not want her to do, or she doesn't do what I wanted her to do. There is an unmet expectation between my wife and me. Normally, what do you do in a situation like this? Probably, if you are like most married people, you have learned that expressing your unmet expectations might lead to even more unpleasantness. So, you just think about it. You think about what you could have said. You think about what she said. You think of a good comeback that would put her in her place. You come up with an imaginary exchange of words that leaves you the victor. Sometimes, after thinking of these scenarios, you accidentally spill over into genuine life and say some of them, causing hurt and damage to both of you.

Instead, what if you refused to think bad thoughts? What if a bad thought came into your mind and you identified it and ran it through this grid:

Does this thought glorify God?

Is this thought True?

Honorable?

Right?

Pure?

Lovely?

Of Good Repute?

Is this an Excellent or beautiful thought?

Is this thought Worthy of Praise?

If your answer to those questions is not in the affirmative, then stop thinking it. Do not be conformed to this world instead by *renewing your mind* to think the same thing that God thinks about this moment, person or action.

In the early 1990s, my family and I moved to Denver where we were planting a church in a suburb. We were poor. We were so poor that we had to live in a rough and dangerous part of the city. One day, I was driving home and as I came up to the house we were renting; I looked around. I saw the gang members gathered at the end of the block smoking weed. I saw graffiti all over the buildings. I saw windows with plywood over them. I looked at the house I was renting and how ugly it was, and then at my 20-year-old car on its last leg.

I walked into the house where my wife was, and suddenly I cried. She hugged me and asked me what was wrong. I replied, "I am such a failure. Look at where we live. Look at the shabby possessions that we have. Look at our lives. I am such a failure as a father and a husband."

She hugged me tightly, then got a Bible. She handed me the Bible and asked, "Where does God say that? Where in the Bible does God say that a man is successful based on his socio-economic level?" I just looked at her, and she continued. "If God doesn't think these things about you, then why do you think them? Who do you think is thinking right?"

Now, she said it full of compassion and understanding. It was not a lecture. It was an exhortation to get my mind off of how people judged success and look at what God thought. She said all kinds of really wonderful and affirming things about my relationships and my character. She told me God's thoughts. I was thinking incorrectly, and she had me change how I thought.

Speaking of God's thoughts, look at this passage.

*Yet we do speak **wisdom** among those who are mature; a **wisdom**, however, not of this age nor of the rulers of this age, who are passing away; but we speak God's **wisdom** in a mystery, the hidden **wisdom** which God predestined before the ages to our glory; the **wisdom** which none of the rulers of this age has **understood**; for if they had **understood** it they would not have crucified the Lord of glory; but just as it is written, "Things which eye has not seen and ear has not heard, And which have not entered the heart of man, All that God has prepared for those who love Him." For to us God revealed them through the Spirit; for the Spirit searches all things, even the depths of God. For who among men knows the **thoughts** of a man except the spirit of the man which is in him? Even so the **thoughts of God** no one knows except the Spirit of God. Now we have received, not the spirit of the world, but the Spirit who is from God, so that we may **know** the things freely given to us by God, which things we also speak, not in words taught by human **wisdom**, but in those taught by the Spirit, combining **spiritual thoughts with spiritual words.** But a natural man does not accept the things of the Spirit of God, for they are foolishness to him; and he cannot **understand** them, because they are spiritually appraised. But he who is spiritual appraises all things, yet he himself is appraised by no one. For who has known the **mind of the Lord**, that he will instruct Him? **But we have the mind of Christ.** (1 Corinthians 2:6-16)*

This passage is speaking to us on how we came to Christ and what happened. God allowed us, through His Spirit, to understand His Wisdom. Once we received the Spirit of God, He revealed both our thoughts and God's thoughts to us. Now, we can understand God's thoughts because we have the Spirit within us and we have the mind of Christ. The point I want you to see is God is working in the realm of our thinking and our understanding. It is mental.

Look at Colossians.

*Therefore if you have been raised up with Christ, keep seeking the things above, where Christ is, seated at the right hand of God. **Set your mind** on the things above, not on the things that are on earth. (Colossians 3:1-2)*

Since we know Christ and are His followers, His disciples, we are to keep seeking the things above. How do we do that? How do we seek the things of God and Heaven in our lives here? Look at the next verse. We do it when we 'Set our mind' in the right place. The word 'set' means to put in place. It is like when we 'set the table'. We put the items for dinner on the table. We put them there and leave them there. God says we are to set our minds on things above. This means we are to think about godly and heavenly things and not let our minds come back down to "the things that are on earth."

One more famous passage showing us how to have the victory in our lives is to be victorious in our thoughts.

*For though we walk in the flesh, we do not war according to the flesh, for the weapons of our warfare are not of the flesh, but divinely powerful for the destruction of fortresses. We are destroying **speculations** and every **lofty thing** raised up against the **knowledge** of God, and we are taking every **thought** captive to the obedience of Christ, and we are ready to punish all disobedience, whenever your obedience is complete. (2 Corinthians 10:3-6)*

This passage is speaking of spiritual warfare. God teaches us that spiritual warfare is a battle that not only takes place in the spiritual realm, but it is also a battle which occurs within our thoughts. This passage speaks of our imaginations and philosophies. Anything in our minds that go against the true knowledge of God. What do we do? We look at our thoughts and if that thought does not agree with what God thinks, continuing the warfare metaphor, we take the thought captive. The thought becomes a prisoner of war and removed from the battlefield. We transform it into something God approves of and that act itself is our obedience to Christ. All disobedience that is punished happens when our thoughts are obedient to Jesus.

Let me go back to real life such as a relationship. Whether it is in your home, workplace, or school does not matter. It could even be social media. You have a thought. The thought you have is negative. It is a negative representation of someone Jesus died for and loves. It is a negative rendering of the event. It contains some sinful or almost sinful response in your imagination. Go back to what we have learned and apply it.

Does this thought glorify God?

Is this thought True?

Is this thought Honorable?

Is this thought Right?

Is this thought Pure?

Is this thought Lovely?

Is this thought Of Good Repute?

Is this an Excellent or beautiful thought?

Is this thought Worthy of Praise?

Is this thought in agreement with the mind of Christ and the knowledge of God?

In other words, does God agree with the content and motivation of the thought? If not, then take that thought captive. Stop thinking it. Do not be conformed to this world but be transformed by renewing your mind in order to think God's thoughts.

I always like to ask this question. What would your relationships be like if? What would your relationships be like if you constantly thought of yourself, the other person and the situation from God's perspectives?

PURE HEART

Throughout the past thirty plus years of ministry, I have counseled a lot of people. I do not think I have the gift of counseling. I do not have the gift of mercy. My staff at my church in Virginia told me I should put a plaque on my door saying, "Name That Sin". That is my form of counseling. My father-in-law told me once, "Joe, you can say the harshest things to people and then they thank you for saying it. It has to be a spiritual gift. I do not know why no one has punched you in the nose." My point is I am not much of a shoulder to lean on. This is especially true in one area. I do not know why, but it really bothers me. It is the sin of pornography. It has reached such a place in the church that, whenever I get a counseling request from a man, I assume his wife has caught him in porn. I am correct in my assumption more often than wrong. How is it that men can be so 'holy' in almost every part of their life, yet view porn?

I believe it is the way we seek to create our Playdough disciples. We focus on molding visible behaviors. Porn is a sin we seek to keep invisible. This is the same reason the church takes a stand against homosexuality yet is silent on sins such as greed and coveting. We concentrate on outward sinful activity. We have focused our discipleship and our teaching on external appearances instead of the heart. If I am focused on how I look and sound to other people, well, to be honest no one is in the room when I am looking at porn. I can maintain my image and entertain lustful thoughts. I can be angry, judgmental, greedy and arrogant.

However, if I am focused on my heart and keeping my heart pure, then there is never a moment when this or that behavior is not as bad because no one sees. My goal is not to look good. It is to be good. I do not want to appear to be like Jesus. I want to be like Him.

This is what you see in the Scripture. God is not interested in our jumping through our religious hoops or our modified behavior. God is interested in our hearts. God places a high emphasis on the heat. God uses the word heart 784 times in Scripture.

This is one reason I am passionately against simple behavior modification and calling it discipleship. It is also the reason I titled this book, "Discipleship Of The Heart". I believe God wants to transform us from the inside. I believe that true repentance is a change of heart.

Here is what I teach about repentance. Repentance is almost always linked to belief or faith in Christ. It is a flip side of the same coin. The word repentance in the Greek literally means 'a change of mind'. In the Scripture, when someone repents, they also believe. They stop believing what they were holding to and start believing in Jesus. We see their new belief in their actions as they stop doing the things that their old beliefs led them to do and start doing new actions built on new beliefs. Here is my definition of repentance as I see it in the Scripture.

Repentance is a change of heart that results in a change of thinking that leads to a change of actions.

In Matthew 15:1-20, the religious rulers challenged Jesus for not following their external behaviors. He nor his disciples did the ceremonious hand washing before eating, thus possibly allowing some unclean food particle to go into their mouth.

Then some Pharisees and scribes came to Jesus from Jerusalem and said, "Why do Your disciples break the tradition of the elders? For they do not wash their hands when they eat bread." And He answered and said to them, "Why do you yourselves transgress the commandment of God for the sake of your tradition? For God said, 'Honor your father and mother,' and, 'He who speaks evil of father or mother is to be put to death.' But you say, 'Whoever says to his father or mother, "Whatever I have that would help you has been given to God," he is not to honor his father or his mother.' And by this you invalidated the word of God for the sake of your tradition. You hypocrites, rightly did Isaiah prophesy of you: 'This people honors Me with their lips, but their heart is far away from Me. But in vain do they worship Me, teaching as doctrines the precepts of men.'" After Jesus called the crowd to Him, He said to them, "Hear and understand. It is not what enters into the mouth that defiles the man, but what proceeds out of the mouth, this defiles the man." Then the disciples came and said to Him, "Do You know that the Pharisees were offended when they heard this statement?" But He answered and said, "Every plant which My heavenly Father did not plant shall be uprooted. Let them alone; they are blind guides of the blind. And if a blind man guides a blind man, both will fall into a pit." Peter said to Him, "Explain the parable to us." Jesus said, "Are you still lacking in understanding also? Do you not understand that everything that goes into the mouth passes into the stomach, and is eliminated? But the things that proceed out of the mouth come from the heart, and those defile the man. For out of the heart come evil thoughts, murders, adulteries, fornications, thefts, false witness, slanders. These are the things which defile the man; but to eat with unwashed hands does not defile the man."

Mark 7 has the same story and expands on the list of the things that come from the heart.

For from within, out of the heart of men, proceed the evil thoughts, fornications, thefts, murders, adulteries, deeds of coveting and wickedness, as well as deceit, sensuality, envy, slander, pride and foolishness. All these evil things proceed from within and defile the man." (Mark 7:21-23)

As you look at these passages and see the bad guys, the Pharisees and Scribes, stop and remember who they were in that time period. They were moral people. They were the religious and community leaders. They were devout in their beliefs. People admired and respected them for their morality and education. The reason that we demonize them is simple. Jesus allowed us to SEE their hearts. The average Pharisee would be a well-respected elder in an evangelical church based upon their Bible knowledge and morality.

However, since Jesus does let us see their hearts, we know they had huge problems. Let me restate that. However, since Jesus allows us to see our hearts, we know we have huge problems. When we focus on external morality INSTEAD of our heart, then several things happen. The worst thing is our worship is empty and useless. We are not worshipping and honoring Christ. We have replaced the worship of the true God with our golden calf of pretend. We pretend God isn't concerned with our hearts and our secret sins. We may be passionate and emotional, but in vain do we worship since our hearts are far from Him.

Another sad truth is we become hypocrites. We are not righteous, we are acting righteous which is the qualifier of a hypocrite since the word meant to act. Why is it that out of the 20 evangelical churches around you, 10 of them have pastors that viewed porn this past month? It is because the pastor is acting holy instead of being holy.

The third issue we have is we cannot truly help others. We are blind guides of the blind. We lead other people to fall into the same sinful ditch of heartless faith we have. We lead others to outwardly conform to our religious and moral behaviors while ignoring what really matters.

Finally, Jesus turns and tells us why it is so important to focus on the heart. Look at the passage in Matthew 15 and Mark 7 to see this list of what our heart produces. For out of the heart come:

evil thoughts, murders, adulteries, fornications, thefts, false witness, slanders, murders, deeds of coveting and wickedness, as well as deceit, sensuality, envy, pride and foolishness.

It is from our heart we become prideful. It is not our actions, but our heart, which produces coveting, envy and deceit. Our heart is why we say bad things and have evil thoughts. Our heart is also what culminates in murder, adultery, theft and fornication. All of those outward behaviors and attitudes come from our hearts.

God focuses on our heart because it is what defiles us. Therefore, if we keep our hearts pure, other things such as outward behavior will follow.

How do we get and keep a pure heart?

After there had been much debate, Peter stood up and said to them, "Brethren, you know that in the early days God made a choice among you, that by my mouth the Gentiles would hear the word of the gospel and believe. And God, who knows the heart, testified to them giving them the Holy Spirit, just as He also did to us; and He made no distinction between us and them, cleansing their hearts by faith. (Acts 15:7-9)

Therefore, brethren, since we have confidence to enter the holy place by the blood of Jesus, by a new and living way which He inaugurated for us through the veil, that is, His flesh, and since we have a great priest over the house of God, let us draw near with a sincere heart in full assurance of faith, having our hearts sprinkled clean from an evil conscience and our bodies washed with pure water. (Hebrews 10:19-22)

Our hearts are made pure by faith in Jesus Christ. When we first come to Him, repent and believe in the Person and Work of our Lord, He forgives us of our sins and purifies our hearts. We get a pure heart by coming to Christ for forgiveness. That is the same way that we keep a pure heart. As soon as we discover an impure thought or motivation, as soon as the Holy Spirit reveals to us a sin of thought, attitude or action, we run back to the cross. We confess the sin as God revealed it to us and receive the cleansing forgiveness of Christ.

When I was pastoring Blue Ridge Bible Church, I had a fellow elder and good friend who always used this phrase. I love it and incorporated it into my life and teaching. He said, "Keep short sin accounts. The very moment that you realize there is a sin in your life, in that breath go to Calvary and receive forgiveness." I love that phrase, "Keep short sin accounts". What it literally means is that you keep your heart pure. The moment you see any sort of stain upon it, go to Jesus and have it sprinkled clean by His blood.

Go back to the example of pornography. Imagine you are on your computer and suddenly feel the temptation to sin with porn. In that moment, go to Jesus. "Lord Jesus, I am being tempted in my flesh to look at pornography. I know is a sin. I come to you right now because I have to admit, I am truly tempted. This reveals my heart to me. Lord, you died for me. You gave your live to cleanse my soul and my heart. I do not want to look at porn because if I get caught it will harm my relationships and reputation. I do not want to look at porn because it would stain my heart. You gave Your life for my heart. Father, I come to you to receive power over this temptation and to keep my heart pure."

See the difference? I am not concerned with the outward effects or damage porn could do to my life. I want to protect my heart and keep it pure.

If I have a pure heart full of the Holy Spirit, do I even want to view porn? My heart directs my actions.

WISDOM

I was about to graduate seminary. I was passionate and excited and ready to pursue God's call on my life. I suddenly found myself at a crossroads. I was not at a crossroad of two paths. I had four awesome opportunities in front of me. I had to choose what to do from these four. All four choices were great. I would love to do any one of them. My problem was which one of the 'love to do' would I pick. I did not know what God wanted. I did not know what to do. My wife said she would honor and trust my decision. I prayed. I fasted. I prayed more. I fasted more. I simply could not see an obvious winner or clear loser. This scenario has played itself out several other times in my life. What do we do when every choice is a good one? I go back to what I learned at the moment of my first choice. At that time, I rephrased the question. I asked myself a question which has given me a compass to live by since. Andy Stanley, in his book, "The Best Question Ever", shares his own story and discovery of this question and how it applies to life. I recommend that book as it took my question and made it even more in depth.

The lives we lead are and will be the culmination of the choices we have made. If we make good choices for the most part, we will receive good results. If we make bad choices, we will receive bad results. The key to having a wonderful life, therefore, is simple. It is to make good choices.

The question is, how can you know a good choice? I am not talking about moral issues, or subjects addressed in the Bible. It is a bad choice, a sin, to lie. We need not try to decide on whether we should lie to our wives today. I am referring to other choices. For example, when God first nudged our hearts to leave our church in the Washington DC area and move to the mission field. We had awesome choices in front of us. One decision was to stay in the successful ministry area, with a church body that loved us, and among our friends. The other choice was move to another ministry field and seek to serve and honor Christ there. We were choosing between two wonderful things. We went to the mission field. Our next choice to make was to pick which nation. God had not given us some supernatural sign or verbal call to a country or people group. We just knew that we would leave America and go to a place of greater need. We narrowed our choices down to Thailand or Bolivia. Both countries were great opportunities. All the choices we faced were between goods. Not one of them dealt with a moral subject. None of them were between good or evil. The Bible did not address them. They were all good.

You may need to choose between career paths, moving, college majors, or no college at all. You might wonder which church to join or if you want to connect with a small group. You may seek to make a large purchase or thinking about taking a vacation. How do you know what to do?

The question that will give you great insight, and I wholeheartedly recommend that you read Andy Stanley's book mentioned above, is simple. It is this: What is the wise thing to do?

Once more, since I am a preacher who loves to use object illustrations, let me refer to how I illustrated this in my church as I taught on this subject. I started off by holding four ropes. These ropes were overlapping each other as they lay on the floor in front of me for about 15 feet. They separated, and I tied each rope to a chair about 10 feet apart from each other. Here is what I said.

"Each of these chairs represents the consequences or results of a different decision. If I pull on this rope, the chair tied to the other end of this rope will be the one which comes to me. This end in my hand is the decision. The chair on the other end of the rope results from that decision. This chair on the far end contains bad things. It is a divorce. It is an estranged relationship. It is a moral failure. It is full of pain and remorse."

I asked the congregation, "How can I prevent this chair from being dragged onto the stage with me?"

They answered, "By not pulling on the rope tied to it."

"That is the point. If I do not want those negative results in my life, I cannot wait until they are on the stage with me, I have to go back up the chain of events, this rope, and make a choice. I will not pull on this end if I want to avoid that end."

I untangled the rope tied to that chair and put it on the floor.

"Now, I have three more ropes tied to three more chairs. These chairs do not contain poor results. They are not the consequences of a moral choice. These chairs are all good things. However, as has often been said, 'The worst enemy of the best is what is good'. I do not want good. I do not want to settle for nice. I want to achieve God's best in my life. I want to make as great of an impact as I can with my life. How do I know what to do? All the chairs seem the same to me."

On the back of the chairs where I cannot see it but the congregation can, is a sign. Each chair has one. One sign says "Good". The other sign says "Better". The third chair has a sign that says "Best". Once more, they can see these signs, but I cannot.

I tell the congregation that I want God's best for my life, and I pull the rope tied to the chair labeled "Better". With no prompting, they tell me to stop.

"Why should I not make this decision? All three chairs seem to be identical to me. They all look like they will serve me well." I ask the congregation. They yell back they can see the sign and the sign tells them this is not the best.

"Sign? What sign?" I ask. They point it out to me and someone turns the chairs around so I the signs are facing me.

"That is awesome! So, this chair is better, that one is good, but the one on my right is the best," I say. I pull the chair labeled good towards me and ask, "So am I now going to receive God's best?" They tell me the obvious. I am pulling the wrong chair. I agree with them and pull the chair labeled 'Best' on the stage.

"Did you notice what happened?" I ask them. "First, you had

a perspective I did not. You saw something I could not see. You knew which chair was best and which was only good because you could see it. Those signs were not available for me. That is the first part of wisdom. Wisdom is when we realize God can see things and know things we cannot see and do not know. Then, after I could see from your perspective, or for the sake of this illustration, from God's perspective, I too could see the Best. However, I still pulled on the wrong rope. It is not just seeing, or knowing, what God wants us to do. We must respond to that knowledge. I saw which chair was best and still decided for something less. I had to change my mind and line up with what I knew was the correct perspective. I not only had to see it, I had to respond to it. I want everyone to remember this because we will come back to this point at the end of the sermon."

That opening illustration is a fantastic picture of what true wisdom is. First, let's look at what God says about wisdom and we will create our working definition.

I opened this chapter by telling you that over 30 years ago I asked myself the question, "Is this a wise choice?". This question came to me when I was attending seminary. In my personal study, I read and memorize large portions of Proverbs. As I did this, it revealed over and over how important wisdom is to me. The Holy Spirit led me to do a personal study on it. The Bible uses the words "wise" and "wisdom" 376 times. I highlighted the words wise and wisdom and discovered that God's will for our lives is for us to be wise. Look at Ephesians chapter 5. Earlier we learned that God uses the word 'walk' to describe how we are to live our lives.

Therefore, be careful how you walk, not as unwise men but as wise, making the most of your time, because the days are evil. So then do not be foolish, but understand what the will of the Lord is. (Ephesians 5:15-17)

This verse tells us we need to be careful how we live our lives. We need to pay attention. The key is to walk, *not as unwise men, but as wise.* The result of this is that we will make the most of our time (make excellent choices that impact lives) and at the end of verse 17, we will *understand what the will of the Lord is.*

This is huge! If I want to have a life in which I have lived it to the fullest, made the most of my time; and if I want to understand what the will of God is for my life, then I need to be wise! Wisdom is not only God's will for my life, it is a constant choice I need to make. The illustration is walking. I am to walk as a wise man. This is a step-by-step way of life. I can have wisdom in this step, but if I am not careful, before I walk very far I have stopped walking in wisdom. That is why I have to be careful how I walk.

I emphasize in my ministry the role of the fruit of the Holy Spirit in our lives. This applies to wisdom, because I believe that wisdom is also a fruit of the Holy Spirit. Look at two passages.

Who among you is wise and understanding? Let him show by his good behavior his deeds in the gentleness of wisdom. But if you have bitter jealousy and selfish ambition in your heart, do not be arrogant and so lie against the truth. This wisdom is not that which comes down from above, but is earthly, natural, demonic. For where jealousy and selfish ambition exist, there is disorder and every evil thing. But the wisdom from above is first pure, then peaceable, gentle, reasonable, full of mercy and good fruits, unwavering, without hypocrisy. And the seed whose fruit is righteousness is sown in peace by those who make peace. (James 3:13-18)

Now the deeds of the flesh are evident, which are: immorality, impurity, sensuality, idolatry, sorcery, enmities, strife, jealousy, outbursts of anger, disputes, dissensions, factions, envying, drunkenness, carousing, and things like these, of which I forewarn you, just as I have forewarned you, that those who practice such things will not inherit the kingdom of God. But the fruit of the Spirit is love, joy, peace, patience, kindness, goodness, faithfulness, gentleness, self-control; against such things there is no law. (Galatians 5:19-23)

I have already underlined words are in both passages to show there is some similarity in the discussion. God is contrasting in one passage the life without surrender to the control of the Holy Spirit and in the other one the wisdom of man and the wisdom of God. In both passages you can see the natural life and/or our natural wisdom results in bad character and poor relationships. Then, look at what happens in the Holy Spirit filled life.

You have fruit. God's wisdom results in a life full of good fruits. The spirit-filled life has the fruit of peace. God's wisdom is full of peace. The Holy Spirit gives us the fruit of gentleness. God's wisdom is gentle. The Bible lists righteousness as a fruit in Ephesians 5, Philippians 1 and Hebrews 12.

Look at the source of the wisdom. *But the wisdom from above.* I believe this is like love in 1 Corinthians 13. Love is a fruit that manifests itself through other fruits. I believe wisdom is also a fruit seen by producing fruit. Wisdom comes from above and wraps itself in purity, peace, gentleness, reasonableness, mercy and righteousness. It is a fruit basket of fruits in the same way love is. My point is, we do not need the wisdom of man any more than we need the love of man. We need God's wisdom.

What more can we learn about Wisdom? As I have said, the Christian life is not about what God can give us, it is about Who God is. In Proverbs, along with other passages, God personifies Himself as Wisdom. He is the Only Wise God. He is the God of all Wisdom. Several times the Bible says that wisdom belongs to Him.

But by His doing you are in Christ Jesus, who became to us wisdom from God, and righteousness and sanctification, and redemption (1 Corinthians 1:30)

Jesus is our wisdom, that He became for us the wisdom from God. If I want to have God's wisdom in my life, then I need to focus on God in my life.

This is a vital distinction. Which is it: Can I become wise or can I have wisdom? If I believe I can become wise, I focus on my abilities and on developing those abilities and knowledge. If I believe wisdom is a fruit of the Holy Spirit which comes from my relationship with the Father, my focus will be on Him.

Here is my working definition of wisdom. I have to give credit for the basic framework to the Institute in Basic Life Principles. I learned their definition in the late 1980s, and although I do not agree with much of their teachings, their definition of wisdom stuck with me. I have expanded on it to be this:

Wisdom is listening to the Holy Spirit so I can see and respond to people and events from God's perspective.

Wisdom is listening to the Holy Spirit. Once more we return to the truth. The Christian life is all about God. As I abide in the Holy Spirit and walk in Him, He fills me with His Presence and gives me His fruit. One of those fruits is wisdom. When I encounter various circumstances in life, I teach myself to listen to His promptings and His word that He brings to my mind.

Wisdom is listening to the Holy Spirit so I can see...people and events from God's perspective. I learn to look at life differently. Rather than looking at the relationships and roles in my life from my perspective and from what they can do for me or how they can benefit me, I look at them from God's perspective. What does God say about this person and this role? What does God have to say about this opportunity, challenge or circumstance? I look at the world around me through the lens of God. In the illustration with the chairs in my message I could not see the signs at first even though the audience could. The congregation had a perspective I did not share. I turned the chairs around and then saw from their perspective. Wisdom does this to us. We follow the Holy Spirit and learn to see from His perspective.

Wisdom is listening to the Holy Spirit so I can see and respond to people and events from God's perspective. In the illustration I knew the correct chair to pull, but I tugged on a different rope. The point is seeing, or knowing, what the wise thing to do is is not enough. I must do it. I do not look at my wife and see her from God's perspective. I must respond to my wife in the manner God would have me to since I see her from His view. I do not see my money from God's perspective. I see and manage my money from that perspective. Wisdom is not just knowing what to do. Wisdom is doing it.

HUMILITY

The leadership of a pastor's conference invited me to speak on any subject that I desired to address. I decided I would teach on humility. The reason that I chose humility is I am one of the most humble people I have ever met. I truly am humble. Here is how I started the session.

I stop smiling and get serious. "Okay, all joking aside. I am not being funny at this moment. I really want you to be like me. I am humble and you should be as well. I live a humble life and am proud of the humility that I possess. I want to you help you become more like Jesus as you learn from my humility."

People started getting uncomfortable.

What do you think about my statement? If you are like most people, you have been taught if you think you are humble then you are not. If I brag about my humility, or even acknowledge it out loud, I am not humble I am proud.

Church has taught us humility is the stealth bomber of the virtues. It is unseen and unknown. If you see it or know that you have it then it has failed and instead of being humble you are now a proud person. The humble person must never know they are humble. Other people can see it in you, but if you see it, you do not have it.

Can you know if you are humble?

If you think you are humble, does that mean that you are not?

What is humility?

Is that how the Scripture defines humility? Does your view of humility line up with what you see in the Bible?

Look at an incredible passage. This is one of the few places (I think it is the only one) where Jesus described Himself. Other people described the attributes and character of Jesus in various places, but in this passage, Jesus expressed to us one of His character traits and virtues.

Take My yoke upon you and learn from Me, for I am gentle and humble in heart, and you will find rest for your souls. (Matthew 11:29)

Look at it again. *"For I am gentle and humble..."*

Which of the other virtues uses an invisibility cloak? Which of the other Christian virtues do we not know we have, or do we lose if we realize we have them?

If I realize I love you, do I automatically stop loving you because I realized it?

If I am kind to someone, does it somehow become the opposite of kindness if I know it? I was kind until I told someone about my kindness, and at that point my action became a mean one?

If my children keep pushing and pushing me, but I respond in patience to them, does it mean I was impatient when I tell my wife about my patience?

If I am gentle to you and know I was gentle, is my gentleness now a display of harshness?

If I feel full of joy, does that mean I am depressed?

Truly, which virtue other than humility must remain undetected by the holder of the virtue? Which other virtue becomes its opposite the moment you discover you possessed it?

The only time I can truly obey God is when I think I am disobeying Him. If I think I am in pride and sin, that means I am humble. If I think I am obeying Him through being humble, it means I am full of pride and need to repent. I can only walk in victory when I feel like I am in defeat. I can only make God happy when I think I disappoint Him.

Go back to what Jesus said. *"I am humble"*.

There are three choices.

The statement was false, but Jesus thought it was true. He thought He was humble, but really, He was not.

The statement was false, and Jesus knew it was false. He knew He wasn't humble but lied about it.

The statement was true. He was humble, and He knew it.

Did Jesus have a low estimate of His ability or worth?

Did Jesus remember He was a sinner, and His accomplishments were based upon the work of others?

Did Jesus know He was no better than anyone else?

Did Jesus feel small in the scheme of things?

Let's look at four passages that discuss humility and do two things. First, let's see if those passages teach anything like we believe about humility (as mentioned above). Then, go through the passages and see if you can identify any commonalities to understand what humility truly is.

Come to Me, all who are weary and heavy-laden, and I will give you rest. Take My yoke upon you and learn from Me, for I am gentle and humble in heart, and you will find rest for your souls. For My yoke is easy and My burden is light. (Matthew 11:28-30)

Therefore if there is any encouragement in Christ, if there is any consolation of love, if there is any fellowship of the Spirit, if any affection and compassion, make my joy complete by being of the same mind, maintaining the same love, united in spirit, intent on one purpose. Do nothing from selfishness or empty conceit, but with humility of mind regard one another as more important than yourselves; do not merely look out for your own personal interests, but also for the interests of others. Have this attitude in yourselves which was also in Christ Jesus, who, although He existed in the form of God, did not regard equality with God a thing to be grasped, but emptied Himself, taking the form of a bond-servant, and being made in the likeness of men. Being found in appearance as a man, He humbled Himself by becoming obedient to the point of death, even death on a cross. For this reason also, God highly exalted Him, and bestowed on Him the name which is above every name, so that at the name of Jesus every knee will bow, of those who are in heaven and on earth and under the earth, and that every tongue will confess that Jesus Christ is Lord, to the glory of God the Father. (Philippians 2:1-11)

What is the source of quarrels and conflicts among you? Is not the source your pleasures that wage war in your members? You lust and do not have; so you commit murder. You are envious and cannot obtain; so you fight and quarrel. You do not have because you do not ask. You ask and do not receive, because you ask with wrong motives, so that you may spend it on your pleasures. You adulteresses, do you not know that friendship with the world is hostility toward God? Therefore whoever wishes to be a friend of the world makes himself an enemy of God. Or do you think that the Scripture speaks to no purpose: "He jealously desires the Spirit which He has made to dwell in us"? But He gives a greater grace. Therefore it says, "God is opposed to the proud, but gives grace to the humble." Submit therefore to God. Resist the devil and he will flee from you. Draw near to God and He will draw near to you. Cleanse your hands, you sinners; and purify your hearts, you double-minded. Be miserable and mourn and weep; let your laughter be turned into mourning and your joy to gloom. Humble yourselves in the presence of the Lord, and He will exalt you. (James 4:1-10)

You younger men, likewise, be subject to your elders; and all of you, clothe yourselves with humility toward one another, for God is opposed to the proud, but gives grace to the humble. Therefore humble yourselves under the mighty hand of God, that He may exalt you at the proper time, casting all your anxiety on Him, because He cares for you. Be of sober spirit, be on the alert. Your adversary, the devil, prowls around like a roaring lion, seeking someone to devour. But resist him, firm in your faith, knowing that the same experiences of suffering are being accomplished by your brethren who are in the world. After you have suffered for a little while, the God of all grace, who called you to His eternal glory in Christ, will Himself perfect, confirm, strengthen and establish you. To Him be dominion forever and ever. Amen. (1 Peter 5:5-11)

First, look through the passages and see where you find your current definition of humility as the stealth virtue. (Hint: It isn't there!)

Now, on your own, go through the passages and identify various commonalities. What do you see in more than one passage. Go ahead. I will wait.

Here are some of the ones I noticed.

Humility is a Spiritual warfare since two of the passages mention resisting the devil. Three of the passages talk about fighting against selfishness and conceit.

Humility is the will of God for our lives. Jesus said to be humble like Him and the other three passages command us to be humble.

Humility has to do with releasing our burdens. Jesus said if we were weary and heavy laden He would give us rest and Peter told us to cast our anxiety upon God.

Humility is the opposite of pride in three passages. Pride is when I focus on myself above others. It can be if I think I am better than others or if I think I am worse than others. I am thinking of myself.

Those are just some commonalities. There are others I did not list because I want you to do the exercise yourself. I printed these passages side by side and then used different color highlighters to mark things in common. It truly is eye opening. I have taught on this a few times in various messages and I pass out the passages to the congregation. I give them three minutes to do the exercise and it is awesome to watch the light come on inside of them as they realize their definition of humility is not in the Bible. Based upon these passages, here is my working definition of humility.

Humility is recognizing the love of God for me, submitting to Him, and depending upon Him to meet my needs to His glory.

Humility is recognizing the love of God for me. Humility starts off like every genuine item of Christian growth. It focuses on the Person of God. These passages speak to the character and love of God. They mention God, the Spirit and the Son. We can be humble because Jesus is gentle. Look at the preface in Philippians 2 as it focuses on fellowship, love and compassion. The focus of my humility is not my humility, it is my God.

Humility is recognizing the love of God for me, submitting to Him. We are to take the yoke of Jesus upon ourselves. We are to have the attitude of Jesus, Who obeyed the Father even to the death of the cross. James flat out says to *"Submit therefore to God"*. Peter mentions that as we obey God, we are subject to our elders.

Humility is recognizing the love of God for me, submitting to Him, and depending upon Him to meet my needs. As I take the yoke of Jesus upon me, I will find rest for my soul. Jesus emptied Himself and became obedient to the Father. The Father then exalted Jesus above all. In the same manner, God will meet my needs and exalt me. Peter said in the end God *will perfect, confirm, strengthen and establish you.* I do not meet my needs. I do not manipulate others and circumstances. I can cast all my anxiety upon Him because He cares for me.

Humility is recognizing the love of God for me, submitting to Him, and depending upon Him to meet my needs to His glory. As in everything, the purpose is to glorify God. Jesus receives all glory above all things. Peter put it this way: *To Him be dominion forever and ever. Amen.*

How does this work out in life? My focus in my circumstances is not myself. It is to submit to Christ in love and trust Him to work through me for His glory. I have something I do before every conference or sermon. It is a little spiritual exercise. It is a prayer.

"Father, I come to you right now with my anxiety and my desires. I want to do well. I want people to like me. I want people to think I am an excellent speaker. I give you all of those desires. Please let me do well in the mechanics of my presentation, in the memory of my preparation and notes, in my body language and facial expressions. I don't want this so I impress the audience, although I enjoy impressing people. I want to do it for two reasons. They need to hear and understand Your truth I am teaching. I also want to glorify Your Name through my presentation. Let me do well enough to not distract from the truth and Your glory. I give You all of my concerns and goals and trust You through Your Spirit to accomplish Your will."

This is not a rote prayer. The words vary, but the meaning is the same. I submit to the Holy Spirit and give my desires to the Father in order for Him to accomplish His glory through me.

Another example might help. Occasionally people will make appointments with me to correct or teach me. An elder might believe there is something I have done wrong or need to improve upon, or a member may have a problem with something I said or did. It is a confrontation. Whenever this happens, this goes on in my heart and mind.

Once more, not a rote prayer, but a genuine desire. I need not defend myself. I need not prove myself. I do not have to show they are wrong in order for me to be right. I just need to trust God to work and give Him my desire to be something or someone. I submit to the truth that He might work through this person. I honestly want to glorify Him in and through the confrontation or conflict, so His peace permeates it all.

Humility is recognizing the love of God for me, submitting to Him, and depending upon Him to meet my needs to His glory.

GRACE

Denise and I were married about three years when she did something I will never forget. We were in seminary and had little money. It was my birthday. She gave me a party and then she had probably 10 unique gifts for me. What she had done is for the last year, every time I had mentioned something that I might like but we could not afford, she would go back to the store and buy it and then she would do without things until the budget recovered. My birthday comprised every item I had said I wanted for a year. It was perfect.

Why was this such a wonderful birthday? Well, what makes a gift special to you? It was thoughtful. It took effort. She totally focused on me and what I wanted. It showed for an entire year my upcoming special day was on her mind. It was costly to her. It was a sacrificial gift.

Those are all things that make up a magnificent gift. It is also why I am opposed to giving gift cards as presents. I think they are thoughtless. This chapter is about God's gift to us. Grace.

Grace is one of those words used a lot in evangelical Christianity. We define it with clever little sayings such as God's Riches At Christ's Expense. It is both ignored and abused. We abuse it in a lot of churches that preach one can do anything at all because of grace, even though the Bible says grace is not a license to sin. However, the worst thing is that most churches ignore it after salvation.

I believe most evangelical Christians do the exact opposite of what God says and instead do what He warns us against. *Are you so foolish? Having begun by the Spirit, are you now being perfected by the flesh? (Galatians 3:3)*. We preach salvation by grace and people respond to it and freely receive Christ. Then, without even knowing it, we end up teaching growth by works. I believe that the proper way is how God used Paul to describe it.

But by the grace of God I am what I am, and His grace toward me did not prove vain; but I labored even more than all of them, yet not I, but the grace of God with me. (1 Corinthians 15:10)

I understand it is God's grace that has made me everything that I am at this moment. Any good in or through my life that has happened is purely God's grace. However, God's grace is not an inactive force that just forgives my sins when needed. It is something (or Someone) that produces action and change. His grace is not empty or vain. Instead, it causes me to labor. His grace produces within me a desire to honor Him through my life. So, I work hard. I practice the disciplines. I do what I can to cooperate with the Holy Spirit in conforming me to Christ. Then, I look at my life and the verse starts over. It was the grace of God in me causing me to work. By the grace of God I am what I am….and the cycle continues. I call it a Grace Sandwich with me at the middle. (See that me-at. Cute.) My life starts off by the Grace of God, it ends by the Grace of God and in the middle it is His Grace causing me to work.

Grace is not just a means to be saved. It is how everything good and Godly in my life happens.

As always, let me give my definition. I believe that when you properly and Biblically define the word, it helps you apply it.

We know and preach that it is by Grace that we are saved.

For by grace you have been saved through faith; and that not of yourselves, it is the gift of God; not as a result of works, so that no one may boast. (Ephesians 2:8-9)

One thing we tend to do is to leave verse 10 out of this passage. Add it and you will discover that it is not only God's grace that saves us…that same grace that prevents us from boasting is what changes us and has us do God's will.

For by grace you have been saved through faith; and that not of yourselves, it is the gift of God; not as a result of works, so that no one may boast. For we are His workmanship, created in Christ Jesus for good works, which God prepared beforehand so that we would walk in them. (Ephesians 2:8-10)

We are His workmanship. He saved us (created us) in Christ in order to do the good works that he has ordained for us to do. This is in the same context, literally the same sentence (connecting word 'For') as being saved by Grace.

Notice what Colossians teaches.

Therefore as you have received Christ Jesus the Lord, so walk in Him (Colossians 2:6)

I received Christ Jesus by grace and faith. So, I now walk in Him by that same grace and faith. Grace is a simple gift by God. It is not of us. In Romans 4 when God is showing that Abraham was saved by Faith, He says,

Now to the one who works, his wage is not credited as a favor, but as what is due. But to the one who does not work, but believes in Him who justifies the ungodly, his faith is credited as righteousness (Romans 4:4-5)

God connects this free salvation by faith with grace a few verses down

For this reason it is by faith, in order that it may be in accordance with grace...(Romans 4:16).

Still emphasizing that grace is unmerited and unearned, in Romans 11 God says,

But if it is by grace, it is no longer on the basis of works, otherwise grace is no longer grace. (Romans 11:6)

With these verses as the background, here is my working definition of Grace.

Grace: God Freely Meeting My Needs Through Himself And His Power for His glory.

I believe that all the components of this definition are at work in Biblical grace.

God. First, it is God initiated. God is the one that dispenses grace. It begins within Him. True grace comes from God to me. There are a lot of theological terms to describe this truth. God's grace comes from God to me and not the other way around.

God Freely Meeting My Needs. I do not earn the favor of God, nor do I pay it off after He gives it to me. I cannot stand the song lyrics that say we are such a debtor to grace. We are not. It was a gift, not a loan. I cannot do anything that will make God give me grace. It is the very fact that I need grace that makes it available. You see, if I did not need grace then I would simply earn a wage.

God Freely Meeting My Needs Through Himself. Please stop and think about this. I believe this aspect is the most over-looked part of grace. We look at grace as simply an activity of God or a gift that God gives us. It is more than that. Our focus is not on the gifts it is on the giver. Grace is not only God initiated, it is an actual attribute of God. Grace is not just God giving me something; it is God giving me Himself. As we have already dis-covered in our studies on Love, Spiritual Fruit, and Wisdom...it is always about and for God. When I need the grace of God, I find it in the Person of God.

And the Word became flesh, and dwelt among us, and we beheld His glory, glory as of the only begotten from the Father, full of grace and truth. (John 1:14)

For the Law was given through Moses; grace and truth were realized through Jesus Christ." (John 1:17)

And after you have suffered for a little while, the God of all grace, who called you to His eternal glory in Christ, will Himself perfect, confirm, strengthen and establish you. (1 Peter 5:10)

The term "Grace of God" or "Grace of our Lord", phrases describing grace as a derivative of God appear 50 times in the New Testament. Grace is not a magic that God uses to bless us. It is not a package that He sends to us. Grace is the Person and Presence of God in my life at this moment to freely meet my needs. As I abide in Him, I find His Grace there with me.

God Freely Meeting My Needs Through Himself And His Power. Grace is not only an attribute of God, it is an activity of Him. It describes how He works towards us. It is God's grace that saves us—His power in our lives. It is God's grace that saves us and keeps us saved. It is God's grace that works in our lives to allow us to serve Him. It is God's grace that....you can fill in the blank. It is grace, more grace, and more grace. God is Present in my life and with Him is His Grace working in my life.

God Freely Meeting My Needs Through Himself And His Power for His glory. As in everything, the glory goes to God. He does not just meet our needs. He meets our needs so that we and others can offer Him praise and thanksgiving. He meets our needs in order to work through us to accomplish His will and to receive the glory due His Name. Grace is not about me. Grace is about God in and through me.

But by the grace of God I am what I am, and His grace toward me did not prove vain; but I labored even more than all of them, yet not I, but the grace of God with me. (1 Corinthians 15:10)

Everything that God desires me to be, His grace enables me to be!

Understanding Grace will free us up to live in Him and in It. When I know that Grace is found in the Person and Presence of God and that the purpose and power of Grace is to help me bring glory and honor to Him, my expectations and my life are transformed.

I do not go to God to find the 'grace to get through this'. I go to God. I focus on Him. He is What and Who I need. The awesome thing is, His Grace is part of Who He Is. So, by default, I receive His Grace just by being with Him. For example, when my son died, I did not try to receive grace to help me through another day or enable me to meet the needs of my family. I went to God with my sorrow and my pain. I went to God with my anger and hurt. I went to God with my lack of understanding and my struggle. I found in the Presence of God the Grace I needed to meet the needs of my family. Do you see the difference? Grace is not us asking God to give us a present. Grace is the actual Presence of God. Then He will see my needs. I may not even know what I really need. He does and through Himself and His Power and for His Glory, He will freely meet them.

FAITH

In 1977 I stood in line to get tickets to the blockbuster film "Star Wars". Within the next few months, I saw the movie 10 times. I became a Star Wars fan. Since that movie, I have seen every single Star Wars film on opening day with the exception of "The Rise Of Skywalker" which I saw on day two.

I never get my theology from movies. My entertainment is from movies and my theology is from the Bible. I say this because it seems to me that a lot of us have derived some portion of our theology of faith from George Lucas instead of the Bible. Star Wars is all about the force. In the movies and the books, the force is always being channeled. You trust the force. You believe in the force. You let the force take precedent over your mind. Through the force we can do impossible things. Through the force we can accomplish miracles. Rey even healed a giant cave snake through the force in the last movie.

I have watched as Christians treat the subject of faith as if it were the force. If you watch some televangelist and faith healers, you would think faith was God. It would appear if we have enough faith, then God has to obey our will instead of the other way around. If we have faith, then we can have health. If we have faith, then we can have wealth. If we have faith, then we can create our own reality and receive our heart's desires.

Unfortunately, the opposite extreme is also present. In my subculture of evangelical Christianity, Baptist like folks and Bible churches, faith is as ignored as the force is by the majority of the Star Wars universe population. Faith is heard of but never used.

Which is it? Is faith this powerful force we can tap into and accomplish our dreams? Or is faith just a door that we open in order to be saved, and after salvation it is a part of an ancient religious belief? What is faith?

I am amazed at how so many of our discipleship programs ignore walking or living by Faith. In the Bible the word 'faith' and its derivatives are used 430 times. The word 'believe' and it's derivatives are used 257 times. The word 'trust' and it's derivatives are used 181 times. Add those up and you will see that God refers to us having faith, believing and trusting over 800 times. It is a big deal to God. Consider these verses:

For in it the righteousness of God is revealed from faith to faith; as it is written, "But the righteous man shall live by faith. (Romans 1:17)

I have been crucified with Christ; and it is no longer I who live, but Christ lives in me; and the life which I now live in the flesh I live by faith in the Son of God, who loved me and gave Himself up for me. (Galatians 2:20)

Now that no one is justified by the Law before God is evident; for, "The righteous man shall live by faith. (Galatians 3:11)

for we walk by faith, not by sight. (2 Corinthians 5:7)

And without faith it is impossible to please Him, for he who comes to God must believe that He is and that He is a rewarder of those who seek Him. (Hebrews 11:6)

God says we should live by faith, we should walk by faith and without faith we cannot please Him! Now, ask yourself this question: What does it mean to live by faith and am I doing it?

I have asked this question to over fifty mature Christian men. Not once did they reply with total confidence in either their knowledge of what it meant to walk by faith, or actually doing it. The vast majority of believers do not have a developed theology of faith. Despite the truth God says we cannot please Him without it, most discipleship curriculums either ignore it or just lightly touch upon it. Usually, we leave faith at the cross.

We are saved by faith, but we do not live by faith. We believe and trust the Person and Work of Christ for the forgiveness of sins. After that moment, how often does our faith direct our steps?

So, the first thing to understand is to define what faith actually means. The good thing is we do not have to try very hard. God defines it for us. He wrote an entire chapter on faith and how it impacts our everyday lives in Hebrews 11. I think that if we look at the first and the sixth verse, we can develop a working definition of faith.

Now faith is the assurance of things hoped for, the conviction of things not seen. (Hebrews 11:1)

And without faith it is impossible to please Him, for he who comes to God must believe that He is and that He is a rewarder of those who seek Him. (Hebrews 11:6)

Faith is a total trust in the existence and character of God as revealed in the Bible.

Faith is a total trust: Notice how firm faith is in verse one. It is an assurance and a conviction. The word assurance refers to a foundation or solid rock. It signifies no doubt. The word conviction is a legal term of evidence. It is proof demonstrated. Our faith is not as it has been said, "A blind man in a dark room looking for a black cat that isn't there". Faith is real. Faith is more real than sight. Faith is a total trust with no wavering.

Faith is a total trust in the existence...of God: This is the part of the definition that really lept out of the Scripture and into my heart when I was studying this. I taught a series on faith at my church, and I spent an entire message, 45 minutes, on this one truth. God exists. Look at verse 6. *He who comes to God must believe the He is.* This seems strange. Of course you believe in God, but do you believe He is?

How much influence on your life did the Existence of God have yesterday?

When you had that conflict with your spouse, did the Existence and Presence of God manage your thoughts, attitudes, words or actions?

How much does the Existence of God influence your financial decisions?

Does the Existence of God change the way you parent your children?

Would your co-workers know you believe in the Existence of God based upon how you live your life at the office?

God says we must believe that *HE IS*. I keep saying over and over in this course on discipleship it is all about God. Faith is me consciously acknowledging the Existence and Presence of God. How do I walk by faith? I allow the truth that God Exists, and He is here to influence my every thought, word and deed.

Earlier I discussed the sin of pornography. Imagine this scenario. I sit down at my computer and there is some enticing advertisement or just a sinful, lustful thought (fiery dart of satan) enters my mind. Instead of arguing with myself over the viability or possibility of looking at porn, I acknowledge the Existence of God. God is not some religious belief. God IS, and He is Present with me at this moment. He does not exist in philosophy. He Exists in reality. He really IS, and He really IS HERE. Do you think I would even consider lusting or looking at sinful pornography if God were sitting in the chair beside me watching me and my actions in loving concern? Of course not!

I once led a youth retreat and in a time of question and answer an older teenager asked me, "How far can we go physically without sinning?".

I answered with a question. "How far would you go if your mother was sitting beside you? Consider this. The Bible teaches that God Is and that God Is Here. God is beside you and in you. He desires the best for you. How far would you go if you could actually see God sitting beside your girlfriend watching the two of you in love? Faith teaches us that more real than sight is the truth that God Exists and that He is Present. You go as far as you would with God holding your hand."

Faith is a total trust in the existence and character of God as revealed in the Bible: Look back at verse 6 again. *He is a rewarder of those who seek Him.* The Bible does not just tell us that God Exists. It tells us Who God Is and What He Is Like. We can know God personally and we can learn about His Character. I believe that the Loving, Merciful, Just, Holy, Good, Kind, Giving, Forgiving, All Knowing, All Powerful, Ever Present God is with me... right now...at this moment. My actions should not be based upon my character, but rather upon His. That is faith.

Faith is a total trust in the existence and character of God as revealed in the Bible.

So, to be honest I have already answered this, but what does it mean to live by or to walk by faith? It means in this moment, in this breath, right now with this heart attitude, I acknowledge that the God of the Bible Exists and He is Here. I orient my life around His Existence, Character and Presence. I allow my decisions, all of them, to be determined by His Existence and His Presence. As I understand Him, then I live more and more for Him. That is called following, or discipleship.

In the chapter on 'Abiding', I asked this question: On a moment-by-moment basis, how much actual influence does the Eternal and Unbroken Presence of Jesus Christ have on your life?

This same question is what allows us to walk by faith. I will re-word it.

On a moment-by-moment basis, how much actual influence does the Existence, Character and Presence of God have on your life?

Notice how true discipleship of the heart is really just a conscience acknowledgment of the Reality of God.

We discovered that the way we love each other unconditionally is to abide in the Presence of God Who Is Love.

Spiritual Fruit happens as we abide in the Holy Spirit and allow Him to fill us. When we see fruit that is dishonoring to Christ we confess and receive forgiveness and then receive good fruit from the Holy Spirit.

We learn to control our thoughts by examining them to see if they line up and agree with the Mind of Christ.

We can live a wise life when we receive Wisdom from the All-Wise God. Christ has been made our wisdom.

Humility happens as we recognize God's love for us (faith is... the character of God) and submit to Him trusting that He will meet our needs.

Grace is the Person and Power of God meeting our needs. It is not His gift. It is His Presence in my life.

Walking by Faith is just another step in constantly acknowledging the Person and Presence of God. It is all about Him. Always. Everything. Every moment.

EVANGELISM

I was driving home from work one day. I worked in construction on apartment complexes while attending university at night. Suddenly, a car pulled up beside me and the man inside started waving me over. He wanted me to stop on the side of the interstate. At first I thought it might be road rage. However, I had done nothing wrong. I was driving my junker car in the far right lane. If he were upset over my top speed of 45, he could easily pass me. I looked at him and the look on his face was not one of anger. I sensed no threat. I pulled over.

He jumped out of his car and yelled, "Joe! It is you!" I had no idea who he was. "Do you remember me?" He asked as cars zoomed by us on the freeway.

"I am embarrassed to admit that I do not. You look vaguely familiar, but not really. Who are you?" I asked.

"I am not surprised you don't remember me. I will never forget you." He said. "Last year I worked with you. I only worked one day. After seeing how hard it was to do the job, I decided to find another one. At lunch, you shared Jesus with me. I told you I wasn't interested and did not believe. We had a nice talk. I did not get saved. One thing happened. I could not get the gospel and the love of Christ out of my mind. I could not forget what you said. It kept coming back into my thoughts. Anyway, I want you to know, I got saved three months ago. I prayed and asked God to let me tell you thanks. Here you are! Joe, thank you for telling me about Jesus!"

That was one of the best conversations I ever had. It was such a joy. I lived on that high for probably a month. I did not remember him nor our conversation. I shared Jesus with all of my coworkers on a regular basis. He is such a part of my life. I have to talk about Him. It is an overflow. It is so easy. Yet, I have found that one of the easiest things to do has been somehow transformed to one of the hardest things to do in the church. We have relegated the purpose of our existence on earth to an option for our lives. I truly believe it is an act of spiritual warfare and we have been defeated, temporarily, by it.

I am talking about sharing the gospel. It is our call. It is our privilege. It should be our passion.

Go therefore and make disciples of all the nations, baptizing them in the name of the Father and the Son and the Holy Spirit, teaching them to observe all that I commanded you; and lo, I am with you always, even to the end of the age. (Matthew 28:19-20)

For so the Lord has commanded us, 'I have placed You as a light for the Gentiles, That You may bring salvation to the end of the earth.' (Acts 13:47)

But I do not consider my life of any account as dear to myself, so that I may finish my course and the ministry which I received from the Lord Jesus, to testify solemnly of the gospel of the grace of God. (Acts 20:24)

For I am not ashamed of the gospel, for it is the power of God for salvation to everyone who believes, to the Jew first and also to the Greek. (Romans 1:16)

but sanctify Christ as Lord in your hearts, always being ready to make a defense to everyone who asks you to give an account for the hope that is in you, yet with gentleness and reverence; (1 Peter 3:15)

but you will receive power when the Holy Spirit has come upon you; and you shall be My witnesses both in Jerusalem, and in all Judea and Samaria, and even to the remotest part of the earth. (Acts 1:8)

But you are a chosen race, a royal priesthood, a holy nation, a people for God's own possession, so that you may proclaim the excellencies of Him who has called you out of darkness into His marvelous light; (1 Peter 2:9)

And every day, in the temple and from house to house, they kept right on teaching and preaching Jesus as the Christ. (Acts 5:42)

Now all these things are from God, who reconciled us to Himself through Christ and gave us the ministry of reconciliation, namely, that God was in Christ reconciling the world to Himself, not counting their trespasses against them, and He has committed to us the word of reconciliation. Therefore, we are ambassadors for Christ, as though God were making an appeal through us; we beg you on behalf of Christ, be reconciled to God. He made Him who knew no sin to be sin on our behalf, so that we might become the righteousness of God in Him. (2 Corinthians 5:18-21)

It is beyond any dispute. God has called us to share the gospel with others. His purpose in our lives is for to help others know Him for His Glory. We are encouraged, called, and commanded to tell others about Jesus. I do not know what this is so difficult because when you share the gospel; you are really inviting people to a party. You are asking them to come to life and sight. You are rescuing them from emptiness, purposelessness and hell. Inviting someone to know Jesus is the ultimate expression of love for another. Ignoring them and allowing them to go unwarned to a Christless hell is the ultimate form of hate.

In my class on evangelism, I like to point out for true evangelism to take place, there must be at least five components. The person sharing the gospel, the person hearing the gospel, and the Trinity. Look at 1 Peter to see four of the components in action. This is how you must be saved. You must hear the gospel and then respond to the work of the Trinity.

Peter, an apostle of Jesus Christ, To those who reside as aliens, scattered throughout Pontus, Galatia, Cappadocia, Asia, and Bithynia, who are chosen according to the foreknowledge of God the Father, by the sanctifying work of the Spirit, to obey Jesus Christ and be sprinkled with His blood: May grace and peace be yours in the fullest measure. (1 Peter 1:1-2)

First look at the Trinity. In order to be saved, God the Father has to choose you. I am not going to get into some debate over what these terms mean and argue for/against Calvinism. Just read the verse:

who are chosen according to the foreknowledge of God the Father.

It is God who saves us. The Father must include us in His plan. Once more, no election debates, just Bible. Next in line see what the Holy Spirit does for you.

By the sanctifying work of the Spirit.

The Spirit convicts us of our sin and our need for Christ. Without the Holy Spirit convicting us we cannot be saved. Of course, we must have Jesus. It was His Life, Death (Blood) and Resurrection that makes salvation possible.

Jesus Christ and be sprinkled with His blood.

If Jesus had not shed His Blood, then all of us would have stayed in our condemnation and gone to hell for eternity. So, the Father elects, the Holy Spirit sanctifies, and the Son shed His blood.

Now, what about the human component? I must respond to what God has done.

to obey Jesus Christ and be sprinkled with His blood: May grace and peace be yours in the fullest measure.

If I do not respond to the work of God, then I do not receive the salvation of God. The final component is not in this passage. It is the person sharing the story of Christ, the good news, the Gospel. God has chosen to give to us the ministry of reconciliation. He has called us to go and evangelize. Look at Romans 10.

But what does it say? "The word is near you, in your mouth and in your heart"—that is, the word of faith which we are preaching, that if you confess with your mouth Jesus as Lord, and believe in your heart that God raised Him from the dead, you will be saved; for with the heart a person believes, resulting in righteousness, and with the mouth he confesses, resulting in salvation. For the Scripture says, "Whoever believes in Him will not be disappointed." For there is no distinction between Jew and Greek; for the same Lord is Lord of all, abounding in riches for all who call on Him; for "Whoever will call on the name of the Lord will be saved." How then will they call on Him in whom they have not believed? How will they believe in Him whom they have not heard? And how will they hear without a preacher? How will they preach unless they are sent? Just as it is written,"How beautiful are the feet of those who bring good news of good things!" (Romans 10:8-15)

In order for someone to be saved they have to confess and believe the gospel, that Jesus is Lord and that the Father raised Him from the dead. How can someone believe this gospel? They must hear it! How can they hear? Someone has to go to them and tell them! Go Tell!

What is it that we are telling? What is evangelism? Here is my working definition.

Evangelism is sharing the story of the Son, in the power of the Holy Spirit, leaving the results to the Father.

Evangelism is sharing the story: Sharing...used that word on purpose, not telling but sharing. It is normal people in a conversation We do not talk down to others. We talk with others. It is sharing the story that impacted my life. It is called being a witness. That is really all there is to it. I share with you Something and Someone who changed my life. In evangelism there are at least two people involved. The first is the person sharing the story and the second is the person hearing the story. True evangelism is not preaching. It is talking and sharing a life with someone else.

Evangelism is sharing the story of the Son: The story we share is not how our lives changed, although we can incorporate that truth into our evangelism. Evangelism is sharing the story of the Person and Work of Jesus Christ. The gospel is not the good news. It is the good news about Jesus. Every year I train people in evangelism. Whenever we have a short term team come, we spend a little time in how to evangelize. The main point of my class is evangelism only happens when we tell people Jesus lived, died and rose again in order for their sins to be forgiven. It has nothing to do with church, religion, morality or behavior modification. The gospel is the life, death and resurrection of Jesus Christ and the reason He lived, died and rose again.

Evangelism is sharing the story of the Son, in the power of the Holy Spirit: The Holy Spirit must convict and draw people to Jesus. True evangelism is not a canned presentation of some historical facts. Real evangelism is Holy Spirit filled and Holy Spirit led. When I am filled with the Holy Spirit, then I can share the gospel without feeling a need to prove I am right or to defend my beliefs. The Holy Spirit will enable me to share in love. He will permit me to answer in love and gentleness. My focus is on the genuine need of the other person instead of my need to be right or my people pleasing mentality.

Evangelism is sharing the story of the Son, in the power of the Holy Spirit, leaving the results to the Father. God is the Author of salvation. As always, it is all about Him. I do not gain or lose any points based upon the personal response of those I share the gospel with. I trust God to work in their lives. A great example of this is my father. I shared the gospel with my father probably 30 times in a 20-year period. He never received Christ. Yet, I would share with him and pray for him. One day my dad came to visit me. After dinner, he leaned back in his chair. I think he was around 73 years old. He looked at me and said, "Well, I brought my swimsuit. Where can you baptize me?" We were all speechless. I asked him if he had received Jesus and he said yes. My brother had given him a book, "The Case For The

Resurrection" and after reading it he decided to place his faith in Christ. The Father had taken all of those seeds and the watering of them and then finally brought in the harvest. Evangelism is a form of trusting God to work His plan out in the lives of the evangelist and the listener.

God has called you to the awesome joy of evangelism. I say it like this. There is NO way you can be a follower of Jesus Christ and not share Him with others. If you say you are a disciple of Him, then you must do what He did and what He told us to do. That is share His story with others.

Once more, and I will point it out again in the last chapter, notice it is all about the Person and Presence of God. Go back to the Great Commission. There is a vital part of it that is usually ignored, and yet it is what gives us the motivation to fulfill the call.

Go therefore and make disciples of all the nations, baptizing them in the name of the Father and the Son and the Holy Spirit, teaching them to observe all that I commanded you; and lo, I am with you always, even to the end of the age. (Matthew 28:19-20)

God said as we go...remember He is going with us! As we tell others about Jesus, He is there helping us speak and listening to our conversation.

I am with you always, even to the end of the age.

Evangelism is not ME telling the story. It is God and Me telling the story! Evangelism is about God in my life and how He can be in your life also.

DISCIPLING OTHERS

I have eleven children. You read that correctly. We have six boys and five girls. Shortly before my first son was born in 1989, I realized I knew little to nothing about being a good father. I consumed books on marriage and parenting in order to help me. To this date, I believe that I have read over 300 books on these topics. Because of my study and also my passion for family, I have taught a lot on parenting. Denise and I have done many conferences and a lot of disciplining and counseling on parenting. One of the first things that we do is have the parents we are teaching examine their purpose.

When my oldest son was five, Denise and I did an exercise together that we have done several times since then in order to refine and redefine ourselves. We imagined my son was a mature and grown adult. For our exercise, we used 35 years of age as our target goal. We then asked these questions.

What do I want my grown child to be like? What character traits and attitudes do I want them to possess?

What do I want my grown child to know? What basic knowledge do I want them to understand?

What do I want my grown child to be able to do? What skills do I want to impart to them?

What experiences to I want my grown child to have had?

What do I want my grown child to say about his/her life in our home? What adjectives and descriptive terms do I want them to use to describe their childhood and our home atmosphere?

We then wrote comprehensive long-term goals based on these answers. We transformed those long-term goals into short-term goals, into our homeschooling, into our vacations, and into everyday living.

Our goal as a parent is not to raise a child. It is to raise an adult. My goal is not this moment. It is how this moment will transform into the future moments which comprise their lives.

This is the same thing with being a disciple of Jesus Christ. My goal is to to help you be a disciple. It is to help you be a disciple-maker. In the last chapter, I misspoke. I said that God called us to evangelism. I did it on purpose. Let me restate it now.

We are called to make disciples. The first step of creating a disciple is evangelism. Evangelism is the door which allows us to walk into discipleship. Go back to the great commission.

Go therefore and make disciples of all the nations, baptizing them in the name of the Father and the Son and the Holy Spirit, teaching them to observe all that I commanded you; and lo, I am with you always, even to the end of the age. (Matthew 28:19-20)

We are to go and make disciples, not converts. Conversion, or turning from sin to Christ, is the birth of a disciple. Imagine in your own home that you have a baby. Do you stop in the delivery room? Is birth the end goal of parenting? No. Birth is what allows you to become a parent and permits you the joy of training up an adult. Rebirth is the same. Rebirth is what allows someone to start crawling as a disciple. We then get the joy of training up a fully mature follower of Christ.

In the church we have made discipleship a theology course. We have made it so difficult. I was once preaching in a solid Bible church to about 500 people. I asked them to be honest and to raise their hands in answer to my question. I asked, "How many of you feel qualified to disciple someone?"

15 people, more or less, raised their hands. Maybe 3% of the people there answered that they were in their mind qualified. Now, remove the three pastoral staff and the five elders and you had 7 other people in the entire church of 500 who felt capable of discipling.

I then called people to a game of follow the leader. I got about twenty people on the stage and had them follow me, the leader around the church while singing "Following the leader, the leader, the leader" from Peter Pan. After about 45 seconds of me being in front, I stepped aside and told the man right behind me to keep going. I waited about 20 seconds and removed him, letting the person who was third now be number one. I did this two or three more times. I then pointed out that within seconds of the game, I discipled someone to take my place. He, less than 30 seconds later, reproduced himself.

Discipleship is really nothing more than following the Leader.

Be imitators of me, just as I also am of Christ. (1 Corinthians 11:1)

Therefore I exhort you, be imitators of me. (1 Corinthians 4:16)

Brethren, join in following my example, and observe those who walk according to the pattern you have in us. (Philippians 3:17)

Discipleship is teaching others to obey the truth(s) that I have learned and obeyed and to constantly focus on the Person and Presence of God.

It is nothing more than a follower being followed. That simple. Look at that definition again.

Discipleship is teaching others to obey the truth(s) that I have learned and obeyed. I am to teach them to observe all that He has commanded me. I cannot teach people truths that I have not learned. I should not teach others to do what I do not do. The first is ignorance, and the second is hypocrisy. Applying this to normal discipleship, to a follower being followed. I do not need to teach systematic theology to someone if I do not know it. I do know what the Bible says about finances. I can teach that. I do not understand the debate and all the arguments about election. So, I won't include it in my discipling. I have learned and applied how to evaluate my spiritual fruit and to keep short

177

sin accounts before God. So, I will put that in my discipleship program.

Look back at this book. How many new theological terms did you learn? Zero. How much time did we spend in doctrinal debate? Zero. How many other books did I reference or recommend that you read? I think one (Andy Stanley's book on wisdom). Why? It is because discipleship is not Bible college or seminary. It is simply teaching others to obey the truths that I have learned and obeyed.

Why did less than 3% of evangelical Christians think that they were qualified to disciple? It is because we have taught that discipling others needs a theology degree or the equivalent. It does not. It is simply following the Leader. It is a follower being followed.

Discipleship is teaching others to obey the truth(s) that I have learned and obeyed and to constantly focus on the Person and Presence of God.

Go therefore and make disciples of all the nations, baptizing them in the name of the Father and the Son and the Holy Spirit, teaching them to observe all that I commanded you; and lo, I am with you always, even to the end of the age. (Matthew 28:19-20)

That last part is a vital component. It is the vital component of discipleship. We are not to stop with teaching Bible truths that we have applied to our lives. We are to emphasize the Person and Presence of God in all things at all times. A disciple is following Jesus and Jesus is right here!

In this book, I have not focused on esoteric or ivory tower doctrines in order to help you feel like you know more Bible than before. I have not tried to teach church history or argue theology.

My goal has been for you to remember the Lord. Look back at our curriculum.

We are to do everything for the glory of God.

God loves you and enables you by His Presence to share His love with others.

Our lives are to be evaluated by Spiritual Fruit which we receive by being filled and following the Holy Spirit.

I must take all my thoughts captive to the obedience of Christ and seek to think His thoughts.

I must keep my heart pure by remembering that Jesus died in order for me to be holy within and without.

Each second of my life is to be lived in His Presence and I abide and walk in Him. In order to make wise decisions I must receive His wisdom and focus on the God of Wisdom.

I can be humble like Christ as I recognize His love for me and submit myself to Him.

The grace of God is available as He meets my needs through His Person and Power.

I live by faith through trusting the Presence and Character of God.

It is all about Jesus. This is not read your Bible, pray, go to church and try to get other people to rinse and repeat. It is being transformed at the heart and soul level as you learn to constantly acknowledge the Person and Presence of God working in and through your life.

Now, as you follow Jesus, go find someone to follow you. **Be a follower being followed.**

DISCIPLESHIP OF THE HEART STUDY GUIDE

I Am Right Here

1. It seems most of the discipleship courses focus on two things.
    a. They concentrate on behavior modification—outward actions.
    b. Read your Bible, pray, go to church and try to get other people to read their Bibles, pray and go to church and try to....in other words, the goal is having a quiet time, attend church and evangelize. The good Christian is the one who does these four things.
    c. Do you agree or disagree? Be ready to share with the others your reasoning and examples.

2. There are two components of the Great Commission in Matthew 28:19-20. The point of this book is we tend to, as a whole, ignore the second part. Comment on this.

3. "Teaching people to follow a system does not mean I taught them to follow Jesus." What do you think of this statement?

4. The book said, "The focus of being a disciple and of being a disciple maker is the Presence and Person of Jesus Christ". Comment on this as you understand it.

5. Read the following paragraph again and comment on it.

"Discipleship is not focused on the past and where Jesus walked. It is focused on the present and where He is taking you as He walks. A disciple is not someone who studied what Jesus did. A disciple is someone who follows Jesus (now) and does what He tells them to do (now). I discovered it is the Person and Presence of Jesus that changes everything. He is not a subject to study. He is the Lord to follow. It is all about Jesus."

GOD WITH ME

1. What would you do differently right now if you knew God was with you? Why?

2. How would you handle temptation to sin if God had His hand on your shoulder at the moment of temptation?

3. Would the Presence and Person of God impact your:
   a. Spending decisions? How and why?
   b. Your choice of words? How and why?
   c. Your actions? How and why?

4. Read the following quote from the book and expand on what the truth in it means to you.

"God is with us. The Father is in us and we are in Him. The Son is in us, and we are in Him. The Holy Spirit is in us, and we are in Him. The nearness of God to us transcends geography. We live in Him. He lives in us."

5. How much did the reality of the Presence and Person of Jesus affect your life this past week? How?

ABIDE IN ME

1. On a moment-by-moment basis, how much actual influence does the Eternal and Unbroken Presence of Jesus Christ have on your life?

2. How often during the day do you think of, listen to, or talk to Jesus?

3. Comment on the following quote. Do you agree or disagree? Give justification for your response. "I think one of the most effective tools Satan uses to keep us from having an effective relationship with Christ is a quiet time."

4. The book stated, "Each step I take is to be in step with Who He Is and the fact I am in Him and He is in me." If you agree with this, how do you apply it to your life? If you do not agree, what do you think needs to be changed in the statement?

5. What is the key to having our lives and our relationships reflect Jesus?

HOLY SPIRIT

1. The book mentioned three basic types of churches in which each church focuses on a different aspect of the Person of God. Has this been true in your life? Discuss it.

2. Read and discuss the following quote.
"I do want us to know the Holy Spirit is the key to living a life that glorifies the Father. The Holy Spirit is the means of receiving God's power and accomplishing His purposes. Most importantly, the Holy Spirit lives inside of you and keeps you always in His Presence."

3. How much emphasis do you personally place on your relationship with the Holy Spirit?

4. Are there any areas or relationships in your life where you are not controlled by the Holy Spirit? What are you going to do about it?

5. Discuss this quote. "The bottom line is that you cannot live the Christian life unless you live in dependence upon the Person and Presence of the Holy Spirit".

SPIRITUAL FRUIT

1. How have you historically evaluated your spiritual life? Have you used fruit, or some activity you engage in to define your growth and maturity? Explain.

2. Talk about what comes out of you when you get bumped. What is the kneejerk reaction in your life when you are bumped? What is it you 'want' to do?

3. Go over each component of the book's definition of Spiritual Fruit. What would you change in your own definition as you understand Spiritual Fruit? "Fruit is the Holy Spirit producing in me, and reproducing through me, the character and kingdom of God."

4. Would others describe your Christian life by pointing to your fruit, patient, kind, gentle, etc., or your understanding of doctrine?

5. "God does not bless me so I will be blessed. He blesses me so I can be a blessing." Comment on how this is seen in your life.

TAIL WAGGING
THE DOG

1. "There is an enormous contrast between doing the disciplines in order to grow and thinking the disciplines are growth." Comment on this quote.

2. Have you ever encountered a spiritual leader like the one mentioned in the book? A person who knew a lot of doctrine and attended church regularly, but whose life did not look like the heart of Jesus? Do you think our systems of discipleship encourage or discourage this from happening?

3. "If what you are doing does not help you, encourage you, or enable you to love God more... why are you doing it?"

4. What is the purpose of your disciplines? Why do you do what you do? Is it working?

5. Do you agree or disagree with the following quote? "The disciplines are a means to an end. They are hypocrisy and legalism if doing them is your goal and not a means to your goal."

DISCIPLINES MAKE DISCIPLES

1. Break the definition down into the component parts of it. Discuss each part. What is your personal definition of Spiritual Disciplines? "Spiritual Disciplines are the Spirit-Led habits and activities that I do in order to know God better and love Him more."

2. One of the areas that can lead us into legalism is thinking the things God has led us to do are the norm for all others. Do you agree or disagree with this? How has it been played out in your life?

3. How can spiritual habits become the substitute for a spiritual life?

4. Based upon what we have learned about God this week, is there anything in your life that God wants you to do. In response to Him, His Word or His Spirit, do you need to change something?

DO EVERYTHING

1. What would be your bumper sticker or tweet to sum up your life?

2. The book defines a successful disciple as "someone who seeks to glorify God in every aspect of their life at every moment of their life". What is your definition of a successful disciple?

3. Discuss the excerpt from the funeral message Joe preached at his son's funeral. Can you find an application for your own life in what he said?

4. "Life is not about getting the 'How To' checklists all finished so you can be super productive. It is not about understanding the deep and profound reasoning behind various philosophical discussions. Life is about the glory of God." Discuss this idea. How does it transform into reality in your life and ministry?

5. A true follower of Christ not only follows Him, but they also point to Him. Do you need to make any adjustments in your life in order to glorify God in all areas?

THE WORD

1. Many times in our lives we want to arrive at a destination without doing the work of taking the journey. Has this happened to you? How and when?

2. What are you doing on a regular basis in order to promote spiritual growth in your life?

3. How much per day do you read in God's Word? Your answer can be in quantity of chapters or time. Do you think the Holy Spirit is happy with your answer? Why or why not?

4. Comment on the following quote and then share if the Holy Spirit is leading you to make any changes in your life.

"God's word is how He has and will reveal His heart to us and His will for us. It is only through knowing His word that we can truly know Him. A disciple is someone who follows Jesus and does what He tells them to do. His word and His Spirit using His word is how He tells us what to do. The focus of discipleship is the Presence and Person of Jesus Christ. His word teaches us Who the Person of Jesus Christ is and what He is like."

GIVING

1. Read 2 Corinthians 8-9 and discuss it. List at least seven things God says about giving.

2. "Giving flows from the living in the Person and Presence of God." What does this mean to you?

3. What steps have you taken to grow in giving?

4. If a lost friend found a record of your giving last year, would they be impressed, shocked or not affected at all? Why?

5. Do you give out of your abundance or out of your joy?

PRAYER

1. Honestly share with the group how you rate your prayer life on a scale of 1 to 10, with 1 being never and 10 being always in prayer.

2. How does your understanding of prayer change if you view prayer as chatting with God?

3. Do you ever listen to God in your prayer time? If so, how?

4. Discuss the definition of prayer. What is your own definition? "Prayer is communicating and cooperating with God to accomplish His will for His glory."

5. "Prayer is not an activity we do, it is a Person we encounter." Discuss.

FASTING

1. When was the last time you fasted for at least three days? One day? What led you to do it?

2. Have you ever heard (or taught) a sermon series on fasting? Why do you think, as a church, this discipline is ignored?

3. Discuss the definition of fasting. "Fasting is choosing to not eat in order to focus on the Person and Work of God".

4. Based upon what we have learned about fasting, is there anything in your life that God wants you to do. In response to Him, His Word or His Spirit, do you need to change something?

GOD REALLY DOES LOVE ME

1. Do you believe, with every fiber of your being, God to-
    tally, unconditionally, and without reservation loves
    you? How does that belief, or unbelief, affect your
    daily life?

2. Do you see God's love as proven or on trial?

3. Joe shared this from his journey of his son's death. "God
    will not prove His love to me by my son living. He has
    already proved His love for me by His Son dying." How
    can believing God's love is beyond question impact
    your relationships?

4. Share your past ideas of God's love. Have you had a
    "God loves me if" view? Have you questioned God's
    love? How can you nail down for all eternity His love
    for you?

UNCONDITIONAL LOVE

1. What do you think about us loving others the way the Father loves the Son and how the Son loves us?

2. There are two types of love, unconditional or conditional. Do you agree or disagree and why?

3. "Love is not an emotion, it is an active force in our lives." Discuss

4. "Love is not just something I do, it is something I receive." How does understanding love is a fruit of the Holy Spirit change the way you think?

5. "Love is not just something I receive, it is Someone I am with." God is love. How can you show others that the Person and Presence of love is in your life?

THINK RIGHT

1. Historically speaking, have you focused on changing your thoughts or your outward actions?

2. How can you offer your thoughts as a sacrifice for the glory of God?

3. How can you take your thoughts captive to the obedience of Christ?

4. What do you do when a thought not reflective of Scripture or Christ enters into your mind?

5. What would your relationships be like if you constantly thought of yourself, the other person and the situation from God's perspectives?

PURE HEART

1. Discuss the definition of repentance: "Repentance is a change of heart that results in a change of thinking that leads to a change of actions."

2. In Matthew 15 and Mark 7, list a few things that come out of the heart. Do you see any of these things in your life?

3. Do you keep short sin accounts?

4. When was the last time you felt conviction and confessed and repented of a sin?

WISDOM

1. How can we make the most of our time according to Ephesians 5?

2. Have you ever heard wisdom mentioned as a fruit of the Holy Spirit? What do you think about it? If so, how do you get wisdom?

3. Discuss this quote: "Which is it: Can I become wise or can I have wisdom? If I believe I can become wise, I focus on my abilities and on developing those abilities and knowledge. If I believe wisdom is a fruit of the Holy Spirit which comes from my relationship with the Father, my focus will be on Him."

4. Discuss the definition of wisdom. Do you agree with it? How would you change it? "Wisdom is listening to the Holy Spirit so I can see and respond to people and events from God's perspective"

HUMILITY

1. How have you historically defined or described humility?

2. Compare the three passages on humility and as a group go over commonalities you see. What does this teach you?

3. Discuss the definition given of humility. "Humility is recognizing the love of God for me, submitting to Him, and depending upon Him to meet my needs to His glory."

4. How can this new understanding of humility be applied to your relationships?

GRACE

1. What makes a gift special to you?

2. The book said, "Grace is not just a means to be saved. It is how everything good and Godly in my life happens." How has God's grace been manifested in your life this week?

3. Discuss the definition. "God Freely Meeting My Needs Through Himself And His Power for His glory."

4. Does understanding God's grace is given to us in the Person and Presence of Jesus change your perspective? How?

FAITH

1. Does your religious heritage tend to have a 'Star Wars' view of faith, or the other extreme where faith is just heard but never seen?

2. If we cannot please God without living by faith, has your last month been pleasing to God? How?

3. Discuss the definition: "Faith is a total trust in the existence and character of God as revealed in the Bible."

4. How have you walked by faith? Is there anything God wants you to do after reading this study?

EVANGELISM

1. When was the last time you shared Christ with someone? Share your story.

2. Why do you think evangelism is almost never done by Christians?

3. What do you think of the book's teaching that salvation requires five persons?

4. Discuss the definition: "Evangelism is sharing the story of the Son, in the power of the Holy Spirit, leaving the results to the Father."

5. Does thinking about the truth that evangelism is not ME telling the story, it is God and Me telling the story, empower you?

DISCIPLING OTHERS

1. What is the goal of your discipleship?

2. Is discipleship hard or easy? Why do you say that?

3. Discuss the definition in detail: "Discipleship is teaching others to obey the truth(s) that I have learned and obeyed and to constantly focus on the Person and Presence of God."

4. Who can you disciple by taking them through this book? When will you ask them and when will you begin?

ABOUT THE AUTHOR

Joe Holman

Joe has been married to his best friend since 1984. Together they have raised 11 children. Joe has been in pastoral ministry since 1988. He has been a church planter, pastor and iin 2007 he and his family moved to the mission field. Joe has a BA in Business from University of Texas and an Masters of Divinity from Southwestern Theological Seminary.

Made in the USA
Middletown, DE
11 June 2021

41730319R00117